100 things guys need to know

by bill zimmerman

ILLUSTRATED BY TYLER PAGE

free spirit
PUBLiSHiNG®

Helping kids
help themselves™
since 1983

Library of Congress Cataloging-in-Publication Data
Zimmerman, William, 1941–
 100 things guys need to know / by Bill Zimmerman ; illustrated by Tyler Page.
   p. cm.
 ISBN 1-57542-167-4
 1. Boys—Conduct of life—Juvenile literature. I. Page, Tyler, 1976- II. Title.
 BJ1641.Z56 2005
 170'.835'1—dc22   2005003369

The names of the young people quoted throughout this book have been changed to protect their privacy.

Edited by Douglas J. Fehlen
Cover design by Marieka Heinlen
Interior design by Percolator
Index by Pamela Van Huss

10 9 8 7 6 5 4 3
Printed in the United States of America

Free Spirit Publishing Inc.
217 Fifth Avenue North, Suite 200
Minneapolis, MN 55401-1299
(612) 338-2068
help4kids@freespirit.com
www.freespirit.com

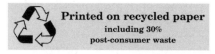

Dedication

This book is dedicated to my beloved father and brother, my dear friend Bob, and all the many children in my life.

Acknowledgments

I wish to acknowledge with appreciation the hard, skillful work of my editor, Douglas Fehlen, in helping me shape and organize this book, and for the research and writing he provided for the supporting material accompanying the readings and for the book's comic pages. I'm also grateful to my publisher, Judy Galbraith, for the encouragement she gave me when I first told her about my vision for this work, and for her ongoing support as the book evolved.

CONTENTS

DEAR READER

Have you ever had questions about how a guy is "supposed" to act? Or wanted some advice on school, friendships, or your future? Chances are, you have. Most guys have lots of questions about getting older.

Adolescence comes with some great perks. You're becoming more independent and gaining new privileges—like spending more time with friends and joining new activities. At the same time, life can seem more complicated. You probably have more responsibilities at home and school. Peer pressure, cliques, and new relationships can make social life confusing. Body changes and differences in the way you think and feel during puberty can leave you wondering, "What's going on with me?" Worrying about the things that come with getting older is natural.

Outside of school, there are a lot of messages about what it means to be a guy. Movies, TV, music, magazines, and other media often hype guys who are buff, tough, and always in control. Sometimes the message is that guys should keep their thoughts and feelings to themselves—that "real guys" don't cry, show emotion, or ask for help—even when they're struggling.

Some guys feel like they have to live up to these images. But you don't have to. More guys are learning that they can figure out for themselves just what kind of male they want to be. Guys are

reaching out to family members, other adults, and friends for help and advice during the ups and downs of adolescence. There's a lot to figure out, and no rulebook with all the right answers. This book can answer some of your questions, but it can also feel good to talk with someone you trust about things you're trying to figure out.

I know from experience that *not* talking about feelings or problems can make adolescence especially hard. My father died when I was young and I missed out on a lot of the advice, support, and encouragement that he could have given me. One day many years later, near the anniversary of his death, I especially missed him. To make myself feel better, I wrote a letter—from him to me. In the letter, I had him "say" some of the things I wanted to hear from him when I was growing up—that he loved me and was proud of me.

Writing that letter made me feel better. It also encouraged me to write this book.

I realized that nearly every guy has questions about getting older. I thought a book with some of the things I've learned in my life could help other guys—guys like you—in their lives.

I imagined writing the book that I could have used growing up. But because a lot has changed since I was young, I decided to ask the experts—boys ages 9–13—what it means to grow up as a boy right now. I sent out a survey to over 500 boys asking all sorts of questions about what it's like to be a guy. (The Guy Survey is reprinted on pages 114–115.) Results and quotes from the survey appear throughout this book. Guys offered thoughts and questions that helped me make sure that I was getting at what was most on their minds, and so I decided to organize the book into sections based on topics they brought up. Here's what you'll find in the sections:

YOU

Answers to questions about what being a guy is all about.
(page 6)

BODY AND MIND

Information on the changes your body and brain go through during adolescence, and ideas for staying in top form.
(page 21)

FAMILY

Ways you can relate to your family and deal with hard times that may come up at home.
(page 42)

SCHOOL

Ideas for making school more fun and meaningful, following your interests, and developing good work habits.
(page 61)

RELATIONSHIPS

Advice for surviving the changing social scene, including tips for dealing with cliques, bullies, and problems with friends.
(page 79)

FUTURE

Practical ideas for things you can do today to prepare for success tomorrow.
(page 96)

Each section has readings with information and advice for different situations. You can think of these readings as letters from me to you—the lowdown from one guy to another. You'll also find a lot of sidebars in the book:

A GUY LIKE YOU

Read about well-known and respected guys who have gone through some of the same situations you might run into.

Take Action!

Find opportunities to think about topics, practice new skills, or write in a journal. (You can also use Post-it® Notes and stick them to the page you're writing about.)

FACT:

Get background information on guy-related issues.

SURVEY SAYS...

Find quotes and info from the Guy Survey.

CHECK THESE OUT

Get the scoop on books and Web sites where you can find more information.

TIPS

Find practical advice and words you can use for specific situations.

Use this book in whatever way works for you. Page through and see what especially interests you. Carry it around with you and look at it from time to time when you need an arm around your shoulder, have questions, or are thinking things through. I know from experience that the road through adolescence has lots of bumps and turns. I hope my words—and those of boys from the survey—are helpful to you on your journey.

Yours in friendship and good will,

Bill Zimmerman

P.S. If you have any good advice, thoughts, or questions of your own, I'd welcome hearing from you. Also feel free to photocopy, fill out, and send the Guy Survey. Send letters or surveys to:

Bill Zimmerman
c/o Free Spirit Publishing
217 Fifth Avenue North, Suite 200
Minneapolis, MN 55401-1299

Or email me at: help4kids@freespirit.com

10 MACHO MYTHS

THEY'RE NOT TRUE!

GUYS *NEVER CRY*

Grandpa's sick.

Mom lost her job.

Ali will never be my friend again after what I said.

But I'm fine... really.

GUYS NEED TO BE BUFF AND TOUGH

(yawn)

... 8, 9, and 10!

IT'S COOL WHEN GUYS DISRESPECT OTHERS

Geez... Is she talking to me?!

GUYS SHOULD ONLY DO "GUY STUFF"

HA HA HA

GUYS AREN'T SUPPOSED TO ASK FOR HELP AND THEY DON'T WORK WELL WITH OTHERS

Really – I got it under control.

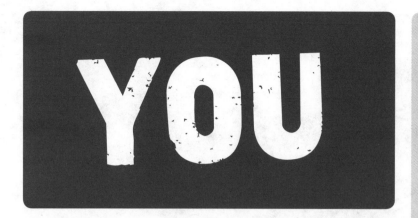

YOU

IT'S MOST IMPORTANT FOR A GUY TO BE:

funny

friendly

IT'S VERY IMPORTANT TO BE:

smart, loyal, brave

IT'S ALSO COOL TO BE:

helpful	polite
strong	creative
confident	independent
sincere	sensitive
kind	patient
loving	fair
attractive	

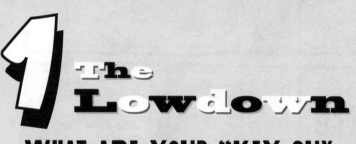

1 The Lowdown

WHAT ARE YOUR "KEY GUY OPERATING PRINCIPLES"?

> "Strive for the best in everything you do."
> —Sam, 12

> "I think guys should just be themselves and not follow others. Forge your own path."
> —Alberto, 13

Like Sam and Alberto, every guy has things that are important to him. Over the years, I figured out that I had some basic things I believed in, too. Things like: **Always try to do your best. Believe in yourself. Be kind to others; treat them as you want to be treated. Keep hope alive in your heart. Work hard to make your dreams come true.** I call these my key operating principles. They helped me as I grew up and have guided me throughout my life.

You probably have some of your own key operating principles. Maybe they're ideas about how a guy should think and act, or qualities you believe it's important to have. Boys who participated in the nationwide Guy Survey (see pages 114–115) talked about what was important to them.

> What do you think it's most important for a guy to be? Take a minute to write down your own key operating principles in a notebook or on Post-it Notes.

6

2 YOU'RE IN THE DRIVER'S SEAT

Maybe you're a guy with a pretty clear idea of what's important to you. Still, growing up isn't always easy. Lots of things are changing at school, at home, and with friends. Maybe you sometimes feel like you're on an unfamiliar road with no map. Life can seem pretty confusing. You may wonder if you're on the right path, and you might worry about taking wrong turns.

With lots of pressures, it's easy to lose sight of where you want to go. But you can keep yourself headed in the right direction. In each new situation you face, ask yourself what YOU want to do. That doesn't mean you have to drive solo. When you're in a tough spot or have a hard decision to make, you've got people you can count on to help point the way: family adults, brothers and sisters, teachers, friends, and others you trust.

Take Action!

Make a list of people you trust. Write down their phone numbers and email addresses so you can get in touch. Keep the list in a handy place where you can always find it.

3 YOU'RE NOT IN THIS ALONE

Look around you at school and you'll see boys from many different backgrounds. They may be of a different age or race than you are. They may be tall, short, or somewhere in between; athletic, funny, brainy, or all of the above. No matter how different from you they may seem, they all have thoughts and feelings just like you do. Deep down, guys worry about many of the same kinds of things: school, grades, sports, family issues, puberty, peer pressure, girls, growing up, and more. It may feel good to know that most guys are going through what you are. You're not alone.

A GUY LIKE YOU

The character of Spider-Man has gone through a lot of changes over the past 40 years. While it's true that he's not a real guy—he's a comic book character, after all—he was created as a kind of "universal guy." You probably know the story of Peter Parker, an ordinary boy who is clumsy, afraid of heights, and lacking athletic ability. Peter is used to going through life pretty much alone. In school he's an outcast. Other guys think he's a wimp, and girls think he's too quiet. When he tries to make friends, people make fun of him. His life suddenly changes when a spider bite gives him powers he never had before.

Spider-Man's creator, **STAN LEE**, wanted to make a comic that young people could relate to. So it's no wonder that Stan showed Parker as an awkward guy dealing with all the regular things adolescents face. Generations of boys have grown up identifying with Peter Parker and wishing for powers of their own. While you'll never have the ability to shoot webs from your wrists, you can build skills that will help you succeed as an adult. And that's a pretty powerful thing.

OTHER GUYS FEEL THE WAY YOU DO

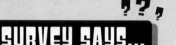
SURVEY SAYS...

"It's hard to just run around and tell people your feelings. It's like YOUR information, and adults don't always understand."
—Rasheed, 12

"I worry about what my friends think of me. Are they talking behind my back?"
—Aaron, 13

"I don't know how to talk to girls. Will I ever have a girlfriend?"
—Latrell, 11

"I'm worried I'm never going to grow."
—Juan, 12

"We might lose our house."
—Peter, 11

"I'm overweight."
—Umberto, 12

"How do I calm myself down?"
—Oscar, 13

"I'm afraid my mom will die from smoking."
—Ted, 10

"I'm always worried about how I look—my hair, my clothes, everything."
—Donovan, 11

"I have trouble with big projects and oral presentations at school."
—Curtis, 12

"Sometimes the wrong people try to influence me."
—Josh, 13

"I'm afraid my parents will get divorced."
—Jackson, 12

"My dad works too much and I don't get to see him."
—Lee, 9

"My grades aren't very good, and I have too much homework."
—Chad, 10

YOU HAVE THE POWER

When I was young, I had a lot of the same worries that guys mentioned in the survey. Sometimes it even felt like I didn't have any say in what was important to me. It seemed that adults made all the decisions and set too many rules about what I could or couldn't do. My dream was to someday work in an office on the top floor of a skyscraper and be in charge of something. I imagined I'd be a big success and make important decisions—all of them right—and that would make me powerful. I later realized that power isn't about having a big office. It's really about the actions that each of us can take to make a positive difference in our lives and the lives of others.

Right now, you have the power to do something good for yourself. Maybe it's hanging out with a buddy or talking something through with your dad. There are things you can do to help someone else, too. You could make dinner for your mom after she's had a long day. Or you could comfort a friend who's dealing with a big problem. Helping others out, showing that you care for them, can make you feel good, too. You may not have *all* of the power and independence you'd like, but you do actually have a lot of control over what happens around you. Your power is in what you decide to do for others and for yourself.

What's one positive difference you can make in your life right now?

CHECK THESE OUT

Boys Know It All by Boys Just Like You. The scoop on everything from girls to grub. Real-life advice on all kinds of situations from 32 boys ages 7–16.

It's My Life (pbskids.org/itsmylife). Information on friends, family, school, and more. Find out what other guys have to say about the ups and downs that come with getting older.

GUYS HAVE "GUY STUFF" TO THINK ABOUT

6

I grew up in a time when most males—including my dad—felt that they had to act in certain ways to be "manly." At that time, dads were supposed to be the ones who worked a job to support the family, while many moms stayed home to take care of the home and children. Men were supposed to act in control, and most men wouldn't talk about their emotions. You weren't a "real man" unless you always showed strength and kept it all together.

Even though times have changed, some of these old ideas are still hanging around. Have you ever noticed how many of the dads on TV programs are shown as not having a clue about raising kids? Or think about the last time you went to an action/adventure movie. What was the male hero like? Maybe he was tough, aggressive, or even disrespectful to women. Messages like these from TV and movies can make this guy stuff pretty confusing. You might wonder, "What is being a man really about?"

In fact, ideas about what a male should do and be have changed a lot since my dad's day. For example, many men today are more involved in raising their children and helping with chores at home. Not only that, but most men no longer think they have to fit the manly mold from the past by hiding what they're feeling. A real man today is simply a guy doing his best for himself and the people he cares about.

FACT: A study from Children NOW, a national organization that works to improve the lives of young people, looked at male characters on television. It found that nearly three-fourths of men on programs acted in an antisocial way. Most of the time the behavior was insulting another character. Men also lied, acted violently (with and without weapons), defied authority, argued, and swore.

Take Action!

Think about the men you respect—like your dad (or another guy who helps take care of you), your teachers, and your coaches. What do you admire in them? Write down your thoughts on the kind of man you want to be when you get older.

CHECK THESE OUT

From Boys to Men by Michael Gurian. Straight answers—just for guys—on tough questions that come with getting older.

KidsHealth (www.kidshealth.com). The Web site with info on growing up, dealing with feelings, and getting along with family and friends.

The Lowdown

IT'S ALL ABOUT BEING YOURSELF

Being a teen guy has plenty of challenges. There are lots of ideas about what teenage boys are "supposed" to be like. Think of movies and TV shows. Lots of times, guys are shown as only interested in sports, chasing girls, or picking on weaker kids.

These images are called *stereotypes*, and you've probably seen plenty of them: the *macho man*, the *nerd*, the *geek*, the *jock*, and so on. But stereotypes aren't true. For example, you can be into sports *and* school, not just one or the other. You can like girls as friends (or more), without being the kind of guy who comes on too strong. And just because you're a guy doesn't mean you have to be tough or have an attitude to show how "manly" you are.

I grew up worrying whether I was macho and tough enough. Did I have what it took to be a man? I remember spending hours lifting weights to bulk up and look more manly. That's why I was impressed that boys who took my survey said that it was important for guys to be kind, sensitive, sincere, and loving. I agree. The strongest guys I know are those who think for themselves and treat everyone with respect. The only big muscle you really need is a good heart.

You're probably still thinking about the kind of guy *you* are, and that's natural. It's all part of growing up. There's one important requirement for being a real guy: be yourself.

THE "BOY CODE"

A psychologist named William Pollack has researched how boys grow up today. He has come up with what he calls the "boy code." It describes a set of unwritten "rules" that guys feel they have to follow. These aren't real rules—like those at home or school. Instead, they're ideas guys pick up on through years of watching friends, family members, other adults, and the media (TV, movies, computer games). These mistaken rules are kind of like habits you don't notice because you've had them so long.

THE "BOY CODE" SAYS GUYS:

1. should be aggressive and violent

2. shouldn't ask for help or show weakness

3. shouldn't do anything that might be seen as "girlish"

4. need to keep their feelings inside

5. need to dominate every situation

The problem with the code is that it doesn't let you be who you are. Instead, it tells you to follow common stereotypes. But you don't have to play the game. You can set your own personal rules for being who you want to be.

Think about your own code. What are some of the rules you have for living your life?

8 LOTS OF GUYS AREN'T BUYING THE MACHO MYTHS

"I'm just not the manly and tough kind of guy."
—Randall, 10

"My friends and I don't care who is 'buffer' than who or who is the toughest. We just like to have fun."
—Trevor, 13

"I'm already pretty confident in myself. I don't need to act tough just to be cool."
—Bob, 13

SURVEY SAYS...

"I know the pressure to be 'manly' is there, and I think a lot of guys feel it. But I feel I don't have anything to prove."
—Antonio, 12

"I've felt pressure to act tough. When I look back it just seems stupid to me."
—Akira, 13

"When someone has to try to act cool it means they're not."
—Phillipé, 10

"All the people at my school are cool and don't tempt me to do anything mean."
—Bill, 11

"You shouldn't be forced to be 'manly' if you don't want to be. Your heart will guide you through any problem like that."
—Tom, 13

"Any time anyone is showing off I usually don't care. I don't need the publicity."
—Nate, 11

"Sometimes someone will tell me to kick the crap out of somebody. I just say no because they haven't done anything to me."
—Dave, 12

"If someone pushes me, people sometimes go, 'Are you gonna let him do that?' I just walk away."
—Dan, 12

MISTAKES ARE OKAY

One of the Macho Myths is that guys shouldn't make mistakes—or admit to them. Some guys worry that not doing something right—say a math problem or something on the field—means they've "failed." Maybe you feel you have to be perfect the first time you do something new. Forget that: there's no need to put such heavy pressure on yourself. There's a reason pencils have erasers. No one does everything right the first time every time—and everyone makes mistakes. Why try to be the exception to that? Slow down and take things a step at a time. Some skills will come easy to you, but others may take a lot of work. When you're learning something new, step by difficult step, be patient with yourself. You'll come through if you keep working hard.

9

Take Action!

Think of something that took you a long time to get the hang of or succeed at. Did you get frustrated along the way? What made you refuse to give up? How did you feel when you finally accomplished your goal? If you want to, write about it. Keep the words as a reminder as you set new goals.

A GUY LIKE YOU

TONY HAWK, one of the most famous skateboarders in the history of the sport, started skating when he was six years old. He was a skinny kid, but he often competed against guys much older and heavier than he was. That didn't stop him from winning tournaments at a young age.

With all his success, there was still one trick that even Tony couldn't pull off—the 900. Tony tried and tried to land it for years. Countless mistakes didn't make him give up. At the 1999 X Games, Tony was in the ramp with hundreds of screaming fans surrounding him. After 11 tries up the ramp, Tony grabbed some huge air, spun around the full 900 degrees, and nailed the landing. The crowd went crazy and stormed the ramp. Thirteen years of trying, failing, and trying again had paid off. Tony put his hands above his head in celebration. Mission accomplished!

10

IT'S SMART TO ASK FOR HELP

There's nothing wrong with admitting you don't have all the answers. Who does? Still, a lot of guys are afraid to speak up when they need help or don't know something. Maybe they think people will laugh or make fun of them. Or maybe it's because of another Macho Myth—that asking for help means a person is weak or isn't smart.

Asking for help was one of the hardest things for me to do when I was young. I didn't have a lot of confidence. I was worried that I couldn't trust people to talk about my problems, so I tried to handle everything on my own. I realized later that there were caring adults around who wanted to help me and make my life better. I just had to give them a chance—and get past my fear of asking for help or looking unsure.

YOU DON'T NEED TO BOTTLE UP YOUR FEELINGS

Ever shake up a bottle of soda and then open the cap? Soda probably shot all over the place because the carbonated liquid became pressurized and needed release. Think of your feelings in the same way. Not letting them out creates a lot of pressure inside you. It's another Macho Myth that "Real guys don't cry" and have to keep their feelings inside. In fact, crying is something *all* people do at some time. It doesn't mean you're weak . . . it means you're human.

Maybe you've somehow learned that showing emotions just isn't cool. It might have been this way for your dad, and so you might think that you can't talk to him about feelings. Or maybe you often hear your coach telling you and other boys on the team to "suck it up." It's hard when you get messages like this from adults. The fact is, expressing your feelings doesn't show weakness, it shows smarts. It means you're dealing with a problem, instead of ignoring it while it builds up inside.

FACT: Bottling up your feelings can lead to headaches, stomachaches, trouble sleeping, feeling alone, difficulties in school, feeling angry all the time, or having a hard time getting along with family and friends.

YOU CAN STAND UP FOR YOURSELF

Everyone has a right to be treated with respect. Now maybe that's not what the kid who's waiting around the corner to bully you wants you to believe. He wants you to be afraid so that he can feel like he has power over you. But you don't have to take his attitude. You have every right to stand up to him and let him know it's not okay for him to threaten or pick on you. Say in a strong voice, "Leave me alone," or, "Quit it!"

Bullies aren't the only ones who can put pressure on you. Friends may try to make you to do things you don't want to. It can be tough to say no when you also want to be one of the guys. But doing what's right for *you*—not what others want—shows respect for yourself. And while a friend might be upset at first, a true pal will accept your decision and not push you to do things you're uncomfortable with.

If you're worried someone will hurt you, walk away from the situation and find an adult to talk to right away. For more advice on dealing with bullies, peer pressure, and the social scene, go to page 79.

"I get along with pretty much everyone at school. A lot of kids put others down and make them feel bad, but I try to help them out."
—John, 12

"Some kids make fun of people with learning or physical disabilities. It's not right. They are no different from anyone else except that they might need special help or tutoring."
—Anferny, 11

RESPECT MATTERS

There are lots of differences among people that seem to set us apart. You know people who are tall or short, heavy or thin. There are probably people in your school from all kinds of cultural, religious, and economic groups. Sometimes these differences can make others look down on or exclude people. But just like you, *all* people deserve respect. Trying to understand and accept those who are different from you shows them respect. And that makes the world a better and friendlier place for everyone to live in.

Maybe (like John said above) you're comfortable with most everyone in your school, but some of your friends tease or hurt others. When this happens, you might feel the need to keep quiet or laugh so you don't look bad in front of everyone. Stand up for others instead. You might say, "Jokes like that aren't funny" or, "Why are you always putting other people down?" It's not easy to speak up, and people may be surprised when you do. But if you get into the habit of it, you might change a few people's minds about how they judge and act toward others. No matter what, when you take a stand against making fun of others, you'll respect yourself and be able to hold your head high.

Take Action!

Imagine what it's like to walk in someone else's shoes. Choose any person from your school—even one you think you have nothing in common with. Picture what this person might be thinking about or wishing for. Maybe you share more with him or her than you realize.

14

GUYS ARE TAKING A STAND

"Teasing is mean and immature."
—Wes, 10

"If you aren't confident and don't stand up to someone pushing you around or calling you names, you will get picked on even more."
—Yao, 12

"I just want to be myself. I don't want to have to listen to what others think I should be like."
—Bret, 11

SURVEY SAYS...

"My friends and I stand up for one another. People try to fight us or get in our faces. We let them know we don't want to fight, and let them cool down."
—Tyrone, 13

"Bullies try to make themselves feel better by making others feel bad. Even though I want to smack them in the jaw, I don't. I just walk away. If they keep bothering me, I'll tell a teacher."
—Tré, 10

"People are teased because of how they dress, how they look, and even how smart they are. It really gets on my nerves. They should learn to accept you for who you are."
—Nick, 12

"At school, if somebody wants me to do something bad I just say 'no' and walk away. That is the easiest way to avoid getting into trouble with others."
—Karl, 11

"If I want do something, I do it. If I don't want to do something, I don't."
—Julio, 12

BELIEVE IN YOURSELF

Even the strongest, most confident guys have days like this: You wake up in the morning and remember all the things that haven't been going right. Maybe you're having trouble with math . . . and your best friend is mad at you . . . *and* you have a huge project to finish before school break. It's not a good day and you're not feeling on top of your game. Time to pull the covers up and go back to bed, right?

Wrong! The best way to get your confidence back is to *stay* in the game. Try remembering the good things about your life—maybe keep a list of them in your backpack or wallet for when things don't look bright. You're smart enough to take on any problem and strong enough to bounce back from any setback. Having a positive attitude is the first step for taking on tough days.

When you're having a tough time, talk with a friend or trusted adult. You'll feel better, and the other person might have ideas that can help.

A GUY LIKE YOU

NELSON MANDELA, the great South African leader, didn't get power and respect by giving up. In fact, he had to fight *apartheid*, a government policy that made people of color second-class citizens in his country. Mandela was forced to live in prison cells for 27 years while white people ruled the nation. Still, he always kept a positive attitude and continued to believe in his future. He educated himself in prison and prepared to be a leader. When the government was forced to change the apartheid policy, Mandela was freed. Soon after, he became the first black president of South Africa. On his 85th birthday he said, "I feel very happy indeed." Mandela's amazing optimism inspired South Africans to believe that they could live in a better world.

YOU'RE ONE OF A KIND

Now is a very exciting time for you. You're growing into your own person and many new opportunities are opening up to you. But as the Guy Survey showed, life can be pretty confusing, too. It doesn't help that there are a lot of ideas out there about what guys are "supposed" to be like. The good news is that guys are creating their own paths and deciding for themselves who they want to be.

Just think for a moment about this. There never has been—and never will be—anyone on earth exactly like you. Just as nobody else has your thumbprint, no one on the planet has your one-of-a-kind mind, personality, or imagination. You bring something to the world that nobody else can. Remembering this will help when the confusing parts of life sneak up on you, or when you feel pressure to be something you're not.

Take Action!

Make a list of the things that make you *you*. Are you kind? Smart? Confident? A good drummer? A cartoonist? An athlete? A good friend? Are you passionate about things you believe in? Someone who knows how to tell a story or joke that makes everyone crack up? Try to come up with at least five things that help define who you are. Keep this list in your wallet or backpack. It's a good way to keep track of your talents and feel good about yourself.

17 OPERATING PRINCIPLES FROM GUYS LIKE YOU

SURVEY SAYS...

"Don't follow anyone. Be your own man and independent."
—Ken, 12

"Be comfortable with who you are. Respect others, but more importantly, respect yourself!"
—Toby, 11

"Don't sweat the small things."
—Ron, 12

"Stand up for what you believe in."
—Derek, 13

"Be true to yourself and the rest will work itself out."
—Don, 11

"Keep your head high."
—Cory, 12

"If you always follow someone's path, you'll never be ahead."
—Joe, 9

"Work hard in life and never give up. If you put your mind to it you will succeed."
—Nomo, 10

"Listen to people—especially when they're trying to teach you something."
—Terry, 13

"If you can't do something, believe in yourself and keep trying. If you need help, ask for it."
—Holden, 10

BODY AND MIND

CHANGE IS THE NAME OF THE GAME

During adolescence, you're really on the move. A lot of things are changing for you at school, at home, and in relationships. You're expected to be more responsible and independent, and new opportunities are coming your way. At the same time, your body begins to go through a big transformation: puberty. Hormones surge, causing changes in the way you look and feel. You've probably noticed some of these differences in yourself—and in others.

In fact, sometimes life as an adolescent guy can feel sort of like a race to see who's growing more facial hair, who's tallest, or who can lift the heaviest weights. While it's easy to get wrapped up in the competition, what really matters is what you do to keep your body and mind in tip-top shape. Keep the focus on yourself, rather than worrying so much about what's happening with all the other guys. It's the best way to stay in control and make all the changes in your life work for you.

19

YOU'RE NORMAL

"AM I NORMAL?"

That might be a question you ask yourself often during the roller-coaster years of puberty. Changes can feel pretty strange. Every guy, though, goes through the same things. The main difference among boys is the timeline of changes. Some guys shoot up tall early on, while others need more time to grow into their bodies. Some guys start shaving in the fifth grade. Others have only a thin spread of "peach fuzz" on their upper lip until they're much older.

No matter where you are, try not to worry. The maturing process is gradual—you won't become a man overnight. And your body knows what it's doing and the time it needs.

The simple truth: You ARE normal just the way you are.

FACT: Some changes during puberty can seem downright weird. At times, parts of your body (nose, ears, feet, hands, genitals, for example) might grow at different rates. Maybe your feet seem too big (or small) for the rest of you. This is temporary. All of the parts of your body will catch up with one another.

A GUY LIKE YOU

ANDY RODDICK is a dominant player in pro tennis. Andy had a breakout year in 2003, winning the U.S. Open at age 21. His size and strength have allowed him to develop one the best serves in tennis—it tops out at over 150 miles per hour! But size hasn't always been in Andy's favor.

As an adolescent Andy was quite short, measuring under five feet tall until age 14. He grew over another whole foot in the following years. These big physical changes created problems for Andy's game. After his huge growth spurt, he had to relearn skills and techniques he had already worked hard to develop—including his serve. Today, after many adjustments to his game, Andy has a big-time serve and an outgoing personality that make him a crowd favorite and a true champion of the court.

If you are worried about any of the body changes you're going through, talk with a parent or another adult you trust to help you sort things out.

The Lowdown

20

PHYSICAL CHANGES

"I don't think anyone is an 'early' or 'late' developer. Everyone has their own rate."
—Derrick, 12

"Some people grow fast at first. Others don't."
—Julio, 10

Derrick and Julio are both right: puberty does come earlier for some and later for others. But generally, starting after the age of nine or ten, your body begins releasing hormones—chemical "messengers" that signal different changes in your body. You get taller and stronger—sometimes at a very fast rate. Your shoulders and chest begin to widen, your arms and legs lengthen, and your internal organs grow larger. Your genitals—testicles and penis—also get bigger and begin producing sperm. Hair begins growing on your face, underarms, chest, arms, legs, and sex organs.

A lot of these changes are pretty exciting—getting taller, stronger, and more adult is great. The problem is that some of the changes that come with puberty can be annoying. Many guys are bothered by body odor, pimples, greasy hair, and a changing voice (maybe squeaky at first, deeper later). It's easy to feel embarrassed about these things, but they're a natural part of growing up that all guys have to deal with.

CHECK THESE OUT

My Body, My Self for Boys by Lynda and Area Madaras. Get in the know with this book on the changes guys go through during adolescence.

The Yuckiest Site on the Internet (yucky.kids.discovery.com). Check out this fun site for a lighter take on puberty. Read the gooey details on sweat, acne, and other weird things going on in your body.

"I think adolescence is a pain. You have to sleep as much as you can and you're always hungry."
—Sam, 11

"It's sometimes hard to tell if you're going through puberty. I'm a little late and wonder when it's going to happen."
—Hakim, 13

TOP PUBERTY PAINS

SURVEY SAYS...

"It's hard when everyone is taller than you and everyone's voice is deeper. I don't really have a choice. I guess I have to just wait."
—Jack, 12

"My voice cracks during class."
—Robert, 11

"The uncoolest thing about puberty is zits."
—Ben, 10

"I don't like getting hair in places I don't want it."
—Tim, 13

"I have to get new shoes all the time because my feet are growing very fast."
—Sebastian, 13

"I don't like talking about body changes with my mom. It's embarrassing."
—Randy, 11

"I'm not very tall yet. (Only five feet.)"
—Hank, 12 "Mood swings are confusing."
—Ryan, 10

"I am getting too tall."
—Alejandro, 13

"I'm worried that my penis won't be big enough."
—Russ, 10

"I get annoying itches."
—Paul, 11

"I'm starting to develop at age 13. If I can still do all of the things that I did before my body changed, then I'm okay with it."
—Robert, 13

22 YOU'RE GROWING INTO A YOUNG MAN

Pimples, body odor, and a squeaky voice aren't the only changes that might be uncomfortable. Many guys also find it hard to talk about sexual development. Puberty is, after all, the time when your sex organs develop and start working. Your penis and testicles grow larger. You'll probably begin to have erections—maybe at embarrassing moments—because of all the hormones surging through your body. You'll begin producing sperm, too. Wet dreams (ejaculating sperm while you sleep) might make you wonder what the heck is going on with your body.

It can be hard to deal with all these confusing body changes. I was 11 when I had my first wet dream. I woke up in the middle of night and my pajamas were wet. I wasn't sure what was happening. During the day, too, my body seemed to have a mind of its own. I began to experience erections at inconvenient times in school. I would walk down the halls with my schoolbooks in front of my fly so that no one would see. What embarrassment!

I wish I had realized then that I didn't need to be ashamed of these bodily changes. And you don't need to be, either. After all, every guy is going through them.

FACT: There are lots of myths out there about masturbation. You've probably heard some of them: Masturbating will make you go blind. You'll grow hair on your palms. You will damage your sex organs. The truth is that masturbation won't cause any physical harm to your body.

Another myth is that penis size is all-important. No matter what you hear, there is no right or wrong size. And the size of your penis has no connection to "how much of a man" you are. You're male—pure and simple. All sizes are normal, and differences between guys your age have more to do with how far along they are in puberty, not how big a penis will be in adulthood.

CHECK THESE OUT

The Guy Book by Mavis Jukes. All the facts on the changes guys go through during puberty. Cool graphics and clever thoughts make it a hip read for any guy.

Puberty 101 (www.puberty101.com). Lots of answers to questions you might be embarrassed to ask.

The Lowdown

CHANGES THAT HAPPEN ON THE INSIDE

23

Some days it might seem like you can't do anything right. Maybe you wake up to your mom nagging about how messy your room is. Then you miss the bus and have to walk to school. You're already late when you realize you've forgotten your history assignment at home. To top it all off, you get into a huge argument with your best friend.

What a day!

It's easy to get down on yourself and feel a little defeated when things don't go your way. Even on less eventful days, you might feel moody. One reason for this is because your brain is changing, too. The hormone and brain changes that cause your body to grow and develop during adolescence also affect what's going on inside you—including the way you feel.

When you have a difficult day, take time to stop for a moment to remember some of the good things in your life. Make a list of the things that make you happy or proud. Maybe they're goals that you've accomplished, people who love you or make you laugh, or a wonderful book you've read that took you into another world.

Writing these things down won't make all of your pain or worry go away. You'll still have to smooth things over with your mom, your history teacher, your friend, or anyone else you need to deal with. But taking a few moments to focus on the positive helps balance the scale and will put you in a better mood for coping with problems.

FACT: Recent brain research in adolescents shows that a lot is going on in that head of yours. It was thought before that the brain was more or less developed by the age of three. Experts now believe that a second stage of brain development happens during adolescence. New pathways are being formed so that thought isn't tied so much to emotion, but to rational thinking. Basically, your brain is figuring out new ways of taking in, organizing, and analyzing information. In the long run, you'll be better prepared to take on adult responsibilities. In the short term, you may have to deal with all kinds of feeling and moods that you haven't experienced before.

Your mood is also affected by testosterone, a chemical produced in the testicles that is the most active hormone in male sexual development. It triggers sperm production, genital growth, muscle development, and other changes that happen in males. Testosterone levels rise and fall often during the course of a day. Along with testosterone bursts, many guys experience major mood swings. One minute you might be feeling great, the next upset about something. Your moods will even out over time.

> "I used to lose my temper a lot, but now I'm older and more mature, and I know how to control it."
> —Andy, 13

YOU CAN HANDLE ANGER

Everyone gets angry sometimes. Anger is a natural human emotion. But during puberty, anger can be a real problem for some guys. The testosterone that causes body changes can also bring out feelings that are very hard to deal with. Maybe you feel mad when your dad or mom gets on your nerves or a friend turns on you. Someone might dump your books in the hallway or a teacher could yell at you for something you didn't do. It's easy at these times to get so riled up that you can't think clearly. But the way some guys choose to react—by shouting, swearing, or striking out with violence—only gets them into more trouble, hurts others, and makes problems harder to solve. They key is to not let anger take over. Work to be the boss of yourself and in charge of your actions.

The confusing thing about anger is that our society often seems to support the idea that it's fine, even admirable, for guys to get mad and lash out. In magazines, TV shows, sporting events, video games, and movies there are lots of images of men acting tough, violent, and out of control. In reality, blowing up doesn't help. Why? Hurting others won't help. Everyone has to manage anger, and learning how to do it now means that you'll get better at it early in the game.

TIPS FOR DEALING WITH ANGER

1. Calm down by taking deep breaths in a quiet place where you can think about what is upsetting you.

2. Step back from the situation and cool off. Tell the person you're angry with that you need some time to figure things out. Talk about it later, once you've settled down.

3. Get help from an adult. If you feel angry almost every day and don't know what to do about it, talk to your dad or mom, your school counselor, a teacher, or someone else you trust.

4. Get the anger out of your body—not by shouting or breaking stuff, but by doing something physical like running, biking, or shooting hoops.

"I'm starting to feel more like an adult."
—Damon, 10

"Puberty means I'm one step closer to being a man."
—Paulo, 12

"A nice thing about puberty is that you grow fast. My dad used to seem tall, but now he's shorter than me."
—Brad, 13

TOP PUBERTY PLUSES

SURVEY SAYS...

"The coolest thing about puberty is that you are not too short for rides at amusement parks."
—Amos, 10

"My voice is getting deeper. That rocks."
—Scott, 12

"It's great to get taller and stronger."
—Terrell, 13

"I'm closer to moving out on my own."
—Dave, 11

"I like getting bigger, having muscles develop, and getting a deeper voice."
—Graham, 12

"You get more responsibility and become more mature."
—Mike, 13

"Ever since I've hit puberty, I'm hungry all the time."
—John, 10

"I get lots of sleep, eat well, and exercise a lot."
—Alex, 13

"I'm not worried about adolescence, I just want to get it over with."
—Kwame, 11

What parts of getting older are you excited about? What parts don't you like? Write about body changes if you want to.

WORK WITH YOUR BODY

Maybe you're like Kwame and wish adolescence would end ASAP. Hard-to-deal-with feelings and major body changes are enough to leave any guy frustrated and impatient. But there are things you can do so that this big transformation doesn't put a major cramp in your style.

The starting point is to keep your body healthy and strong. Eating well, staying in shape, and getting enough sleep will help you to not only look good, but also feel good. Getting all the nutrients and rest you need will give you the energy and confidence to bring your "A game" to each day.

Bottom line: Take charge of your body. Respect what nature gave you. Taking good care of yourself will serve you well as you take on the new challenges and responsibilities that come with getting older.

GUY GAMES

We're here at the Guy Games.

Jake and Tyler are here to show off the sweet moves they use to keep their bodies in primetime shape and feeling good.

Performances here at the Guy Games are judged with these logos: *Rippin'* means a competitor has laid down a smooth trick for staying fit. *Wipeout* means he's lost control.

RIPPIN' WIPEOUT

Jake's just about to attempt his first run here.

OHH!

WIPEOUT

Jake made a bad move earlier by going with soda and junk for lunch. He recovers nicely here by eating the good stuff.

RIPPIN'

Uh oh... Looks like Tyler's *wiped out* on the couch.

WIPEOUT

Look at this! Ty bounces back from the wipeout by going for a jog. That's going to do his body good.

RIPPIN'

No thanks, man. I'm cool.

A close call there for Jake. Smoking is a habit that's hard to break. Cigarettes, alcohol, and drugs all cramp your "freestyle." That rippin' decision will move him up in the field.

RIPPIN'

Uh oh. Tyler's headed for a wipeout. He's taking his anger out on his brother.

WIPEOUT

Nice comeback, Tyler! Exercise with a friend is a better way to get strong feelings out.

RIPPIN'

JAKE
TYLER

WIPEOUT   RIPPIN'

YAY
WOO-HOO!
ALL RIGHT

What a ride!

You got that right, bro!

That's gonna do it here for the Guy Games. This competition has made it clear that Jake and Tyler have the right moves to stay fit and in charge of their bodies. Let's hear it for them!

27

YOU ARE WHAT YOU EAT

You don't have to have the body of Mr. Universe, but you should make an effort to be as healthy as you can. That means eating well—not stuffing or starving yourself—and putting a lot of thought into what you choose to eat. Your body is growing more quickly now than it ever will. It's important to give it all of the right foods it needs to stay healthy and strong so that you can do all the things you want.

Eating right isn't always easy. Lots of school lunch programs offer fast food or sugary snacks as alternatives to good meals. And advertisements on TV might fill you with cravings for junk food and sweets. Greasy hamburgers and fries may taste great, but they're loaded with fat and calories. And eating too much sugar won't give you a lift for long. After a quick burst of energy, you'll end up feeling tired and lazy.

You may have heard it a million times, but there is some truth to the expression "You are what you eat." Eating balanced, regular meals does help you look and feel better. You'll feel more "together" and perform better at the things you love to do, whether it's guarding the net, playing in the band, or succeeding in school.

Take Action!

Can you think of ways to improve your eating habits? Start by cutting out one unhealthy food and replacing it with a good one that you enjoy. Making even small improvements in your diet can help you look and feel better.

CHECK THIS OUT

USDA for Kids (www.usda.gov/news/usdakids). Because your body grows so quickly during adolescence, you need more of nutrients like protein, zinc, calcium, and iron. Check out this Web site for information on eating healthier.

The Lowdown

JUNK FOOD AND SODA

Eating and drinking small amounts of junk food and soda is okay sometimes. Just make sure you balance it out with healthy foods—like fruits and vegetables—your body needs.

- **ONE CAN OF SODA** has 10–12 teaspoons of sugar in it. If you drink only one can of soda each day, you will take in 65 pounds of sugar over the course of a year.

- **SODA** is acidic and can break down tooth enamel—the strongest substance in the body. In fact, if you left a tooth in a glass of soda overnight, it would begin to disintegrate.

- **SUGAR IN SODA** often leads to diabetes, obesity, and tooth decay in young people.

- **CAFFEINE**—also often found in soda—can cause hyperactivity and sleeplessness. (It is also found in coffee, chocolate bars, and other junk food.) Caffeine is a drug that can affect your mood.

- In 1957, the average fast-food burger weighed about one ounce. Today, the typical hamburger weighs six ounces. **TALK ABOUT SUPERSIZING!**

- Because fast-food sandwiches and burgers are now bigger, they have far more calories. Some burgers have over **1,000 CALORIES!** That's more than a third of the calories a typical teenager needs in an entire day.

- The largest portion of fries at major fast food restaurants has about **600 CALORIES**.

- Americans eat more than **20 BILLION** hot dogs a year.

29

MOVE IT OR YOU'LL LOSE IT

Taking care of yourself is a big deal. Getting regular exercise during adolescence is key to keeping your body healthy, flexible, and strong—inside and out. And keeping it fit has a lot to do with feeling good about yourself. It's also a message to others. After all, your body is what you present to the world. How you take care of it tells people something about who you are.

The great thing is that getting a workout doesn't have to seem like work. There are many pleasurable ways of exercising—from riding your bike to skating to swimming. There are also a variety of teams and clubs in schools and communities that offer fun ways to stay fit in the company of friends. Join up!

Take Action!

Choose one good habit or goal for getting more physically fit. Choose a bad habit (too much time as a couch potato? a few chips too many after school?) that you're going to try to break. Keep track of your progress in a notebook.

A GUY LIKE YOU

LANCE ARMSTRONG has accomplished a lot in his life. He's probably best known for his six straight victories in the Tour de France, a French bicycle race that is considered one of the most difficult sporting events in the world. Because of his record, many people consider Lance one of the best athletes of all time. But this wasn't always true.

Lance grew up in Plano, Texas, wanting to be a football star. Problems with coordination kept him from doing well in that sport, so he decided to try swimming instead. Lance, a fifth grader, struggled so much at first that he was put with second graders! Determined to succeed, Lance worked hard and became an excellent swimmer. And he didn't stop there. He also took up biking and running.

By the time he decided to focus on cycling, Lance had built endurance that helped him win races. Not only that, but taking care of himself helped Lance beat testicular cancer. His path to making cycling history shows that just because one activity or sport isn't a fit, that doesn't mean there isn't another way to get your move on and shine.

"I eat well, exercise, and get enough sleep. If I didn't, I could become sluggish and overweight. And my heart could get bad."
—Larry, 13

The Lowdown

A "WEIGHTY" TOPIC

Many health experts feel that young people are spending too much time parked on the sofa eating junk food. They say that obesity is now one of the biggest problems facing today's kids and teens. Obesity has many negative short- and long-term effects on health, including the development of diabetes and high blood pressure.

Experts recommend a balanced diet and regular exercise—at least 30 minutes a day—for staying fit. Is watching television or playing computer games exercise? Not really. Your body burns a few calories when you watch the screen or use the controller, but not many.

FACT: In the United States, kids ages eight and up spend on average four-and-a-half hours watching TV or playing video games each day. Only about half of young people get the regular physical activity they need.

CHECK THESE OUT

BAM! Body and Mind (www.bam.gov). A Web site maintained by the Centers for Disease Control, this is a great resource for learning more about nutrition, setting your own exercise calendar, and finding tips on getting fit and staying healthy.

Kids' Nutrition (www.kidsnutrition.org). Body mass index (BMI) is used to figure out whether a person is overweight. To figure out where you fit in the mix, go to this site from the U.S. Department of Agriculture.

VERB: It's What You Do (www.verbnow.com). A fun site where you can create a character to compete in different online sports. Then use a zip code locator to find real-life opportunities to skate, train, or play in your community.

31

GET YOUR SLEEP

"I try to get enough sleep, but school starts early and it's hard to get enough rest."
—Antony, 12

"I try to get ten hours of sleep every night."
—Freddie, 11

Most guys have a lot going on—homework, hanging out, extracurricular activities. Getting older means more freedom and opportunities for doing new things. But because of your changing body, you need plenty of rest to try them all. Why? It's when you're sleeping that growth hormones do their work. For your body to grow to its full potential, experts say you need eight to ten hours of sleep each night. With all you've got to do, carving out time for this much rest can be hard. But it's important to find a way to do it. If you need a short nap after school, take one. Work to get things done during the day so that you don't have to stay up late at night. Your body is growing at a very fast rate; it needs rest to grow and restore itself after the challenges of each day.

GUYS ARE TAKING CARE OF THEIR BODIES

"I love my body and do all I can to take care of it."
—Joe, 11

"I feel good about my body. I exercise and eat well."
—Rory, 12

"It's important to take care of your body because you'll grow more if you do."
—C.J., 10

SURVEY SAYS...

"I play soccer every day."
—Desmond, 13

"I get a lot of exercise. I have gym two to three days a week and football practice every day after school."
—Lance 12

"I try to eat well, but I do like some candy."
—Isaac, 12

"I play football and basketball for exercise."
—Cal, 13

"If you're healthy, you're in a better mood and can learn better."
—Eric, 11

"I eat some junk food, but I eat healthy food, too. I exercise a lot and feel pretty good about my body."
—Manny, 9

BE OKAY WITH YOUR BODY

There are lots of messages out there about the "perfect body." Maybe you look at your own in the mirror and worry you don't measure up—or that you measure a little too much. It's easy to get confused about where you stand.

The fact is, there is no perfect body. And comparing yourself to others can be a bad thing—especially if you use movie stars or athletes as your measuring stick. Because of unrealistic expectations, more and more guys are developing eating disorders. For example, some starve themselves (or eat too much and then throw up) to "cut weight" for wrestling and other activities. These habits are all dangerous for your growing body. They don't allow it to reach its full potential.

Learn to accept and respect your body. It's the only one you've got and a big part of who you are. Put the emphasis on being healthy, rather than looking a certain way. If you're eating well and getting enough exercise, chances are that you're absolutely fine. Not sure? Talk to a parent about scheduling an appointment with a doctor who can tell you what's best. That way you'll have professional advice for moving forward if you do want to make some changes to improve your diet and increase your activity.

FACT: To gain an athletic edge, some athletes turn to steroids. Using steroids is not only cheating, but also extremely unhealthy. Steroids have serious effects—especially for teens. They can lead to severe acne outbreaks, make hair fall out, cause breast development in guys, and shrink testicles. Steroids can also prevent young people from growing to their full size and weight, cause wild mood swings, and contribute to long-term heart and liver problems. In short, steroids are very bad news for any body—especially one that's still growing.

CHECK THIS OUT

National Eating Disorders Association (www.national eatingdisorders.org). Eating disorders are not only a problem for girls and women. More and more guys have eating problems, too. This Web site gives a lot of information on the different kinds of eating disorders and where to go for help.

PLAY IT SMART

"I haven't been asked to try smoking, alcohol, or drugs, but if I were ever asked I would say 'no.' The reason I say this is because all of these things are very bad for you, and I don't want to take the risk of going to juvenile hall."
—Mark, 12

It's a no-brainer—something you've heard over and over—but here it is again: Cigarettes, alcohol, and other drugs are extremely harmful for your health. They can be tough to avoid, though, because you're becoming more independent and facing new social situations.

You'll probably be changing schools, meeting people, and having plenty of other new experiences. Many of these experiences can make life more fun and interesting. Others can lead to tough spots that put your health and safety in danger. A friend might ask you to try smoking cigarettes, or pressure you to experiment with drugs or alcohol. Hanging out with some people could get you in situations that are dangerous or against the law.

Everybody wants friends. But the pressure to fit in can lead you to do some things you'll regret later on. A mature guy can think for himself. He knows that greater freedom means greater responsibility. You're on your own more now without your mom or dad always watching over you. It's up to you to take over the job of looking out for your body and your mind.

Take Action!

When you are tempted to try something you might regret, take a moment to think about how you'll feel after. Will your opinion of yourself change? Could you harm yourself or upset your family? Thinking about the consequences of actions is a sign of maturity.

CHECK THIS OUT

Freevibe (www.freevibe.com). A Web site with information on the different kinds of drugs, stories from real teens, and advice for saying no when peer pressure is strong.

YOU CAN HANDLE STRESS

I was 12 when my parents' marriage started to break apart, maybe one of the hardest things any family goes through. On top of the distress from the breakup, I had to do a lot of school-work, help care for my brother, and practice every day after school for my Bar Mitzvah (a Jewish tradition marking the transition of a boy to manhood). I felt overwhelmed. I wasn't sure how I was going to deal with the changes in my family and all of my responsibilities. To get a better grip on things, I'd hop on my bike and cycle around, sometimes for hours. It was a healthy way to deal with all the anxiety and physical aches I felt from the pressures in my life. And the cycling gave me a little distance so that I could think clearly about the things bothering me.

You can take steps to get control over your worry and stress, too. Carve out some quiet time to catch your breath in a place like the park, your room, or a place of worship. Or do something else you enjoy. Grab your board and go to the skatepark. Spend some time with a stamp or card collection you have. Taking time away from pressures and clearing your head can give you a fresh perspective for coming up with solutions to problems you're facing.

STRESS SYMPTOMS

1. sweating

2. feeling panicky

3. faster heartbeat

4. butterflies in your stomach (or you might get a stomachache)

5. headaches—too much pressure!

STRESS BUSTERS

1. Eat right and get enough rest. You can only feel your best if you're nourished and rested.

2. Exercise. Activity causes your body to release *endorphins*, chemicals that make you feel more relaxed.

3. Have a laugh. Laughing has been proven to make people feel happier and less stressed. Chill with some friends and joke around. Watch a funny movie or read a comic that you like.

4. Try a relaxation exercise. Find a place you find relaxing, maybe a park or beach where you can hear water running or the wind in the trees. Sit down and keep your body still. Close your eyes. Take deep and slow breaths—inhale through your nose and exhale through your mouth. Think of something—a person or place—that make you happy while you take regular breaths.

5. Hang out with a pet. Pets are great listeners!

Feeling overwhelmed, nervous, or sad all the time might mean you are depressed. If you have these feelings, it's important to talk with an adult immediately. If there's no one around to talk right now, call the Nineline at 1-800-999-9999. The Nineline is a phone service from Covenant House where someone is ready 24 hours a day, seven days a week, to take your call and discuss your feelings.

KEEP YOUR SPIRIT STRONG

"To relax after school, I watch a little television or read a magazine."
—Chris, 13

"I like just relaxing in the sun—it's one of my favorite things to do."
—Garret, 12

In the same way you take care of your body by feeding it healthy food, try to find ways to fill up your mind and spirit, too. How? Do whatever it is that you love. Go out and enjoy nature. Read a book to escape into another world where there are people or places different from what you know. Draw, paint, or color. Play music, or listen to it. Keep a notepad where you can write about your day or your feelings. Try your hand at poetry or writing a song. Meditate or pray. Think about your life and the ways you are connected to those around you. Let your thoughts soar up high.

A strong body, mind, and spirit are all things you need in order to be happy and make the most of each day. Taking some time to find yourself can give you new ways of looking at the world and make your life richer.

FAMILY

FAMILY IS THERE TO SUPPORT YOU

"My older brother always comes through for me. He knows what to do no matter what the situation."
—Dexter, 11

"My parents and brother and sister all compliment and encourage me."
—Roy, 13

"My dad always tells me he's proud of me."
—Carmelo, 13

"Even when I goof up, I have a loving family that always watches my back."
—Brad, 10

Every day you're growing more into your own person. You may have a lot going on: school, sports, after-school programs, weekend activities, and friendships. And this means you're spending more time away from home. Even though you're learning to get along on your own more of the time, you still need your family's love and support. They're still the people you can go to when you need some advice or want to talk things out.

In the Guy Survey, many boys said that they could rely on their families for love and advice. Most noted that they often heard kind words and encouragement from family members.

CHECK THESE OUT

FamilyFun.com (www.familyfun.go.com). This site has ideas for family activities, crafts, holiday projects, and information on travel, vacations, camp sites, and more.

It's My Life—Family (pbskids.org/itsmlife/family). Information on all aspects of family life—including more ideas for staying close to parents and siblings.

When you read about *parents*, think of the adult or adults who live with and take care of you. This might be your mom, dad, stepparents, foster parents, guardians, relatives, or others. *Family* includes these people and brothers, sisters, stepsiblings, or any other kids who share a home with you.

"My parents treat me like I'm still eight years old. Except with chores. They give me more of those."
—Paul, 12

"My parents are always encouraging me, but my grades are never good enough. What's wrong with a B+?"
—Reggie, 10

SOME CONFLICT AT HOME IS NORMAL

While family can be a great source of support, life at home isn't always perfect. Grades, money, homework, rules, siblings, and chores were all mentioned in the Guy Survey as problem areas at home. When you're making more of your own decisions, things can sometimes get tense between you and the adults at home.

Think about your own situation. You're on your own more—doing new things at school and in your neighborhood—but you still have to answer to your family. It may sometimes seem like you're getting mixed messages. One minute your parents might tell you to take on more responsibility, while the next they're saying you're "just a kid" and have a lot to learn. It's normal to feel frustrated when you're not sure where you stand. Your getting older affects your mom and dad, too. They may need to get used to your growing independence. Give them some time to adjust to how you're changing.

Same here. It's caused some problems. We haven't been talking much – or else we've been arguing. "Family night" is supposed to fix things up. I'll give it a shot.

What's family night about, anyway?

Making dinner, playing board games. It should be okay... my parents aren't bad. It's just that sometimes I say stuff and they take it the wrong way.

My mom says talking to me is like talking to a wall... what's that supposed to mean?

Dunno, J. All I get is, "You have a bad attitude."

Sound familiar? Read on!

PARENTS...

OTHER GUYS' THOUGHTS ON FAMILY

"My family fights sometimes, but we all love each other very much and wouldn't hurt each other."
—Phil, 13

"My family will help me with everything, and if I mess up they say it's all right and to get up and try again."
—Jasper, 11

"I'm worried that my mom and dad might not get back together."
—Alan, 11

SURVEY SAYS...

"Sometimes my family doesn't talk because we are in a hurry."
—Gene, 11

"Half the time my dad is very loving, and then other times he is in a bad mood and swears."
—Carl, 10

"I don't really have the mother support like most people have. My aunt is like a mother because she talks to me about school and stuff."
—Tommy, 12

"My parents and I have different views. We don't really get along."
—Enrique, 13

"My mom and dad are nice, but my sisters tell me they hate me."
—Don, 10

"I get yelled at my share, but my family's pretty loving."
—George, 13

"I don't live with my mom and sisters and I worry about them."
—Jerry, 10

THERE ARE ALL KINDS OF FAMILIES

Different guys have different experiences with their families. Some of us are lucky enough to grow up in a family that's warm and close. I had that for a while, but then my parents got divorced, and my life changed a lot. Not many years later my father died, and I had a very hard time dealing with that. I had to learn from a young age how to handle huge changes in family life.

Maybe you've experienced the loss of a parent because of a divorce, a separation, or a death. It's never easy growing up this way, but in time you may learn that you can build an extended family of relatives, friends, neighbors, and other people who care about you. These people can feel as close as family and can be the people you go to for comfort and love.

No matter what kind of family we have, we all share an important need: to have a place that feels like home.

Think about what *home* means to you. Can you visit an aunt or uncle when things are tough? Maybe a grandparent or neighbor has helped take care of you at some time. Home can be any place where you feel safe and cared for.

A GUY LIKE YOU

Since being drafted into the NFL (National Football League), **DAUNTE CULPEPPER** has tossed over 100 touchdown passes for the Minnesota Vikings. Known as one of the best quarterbacks in the league, Daunte owes a lot of his success to his personal drive and determination. But he's the first to mention the role his family's love and support played in his success. Daunte grew up in Ocala, Florida, not knowing his father's name and having little contact with his birth mother. Instead, Daunte found a home in the family of Emma Culpepper. A foster mother to 15 children over the years, Emma Culpepper taught Daunte the importance of family from a young age. It's not surprising this amazing quarterback looks back to where it all began—the loving Culpepper home—when talking about his success in the NFL.

YOU CAN REACH OUT AND CONNECT

"Sometimes my parents are in a bad mood or sad and don't really say much. I try to cheer them up."
—Darryl, 12

It's very normal to have mixed-up feelings about your family sometimes. There are days when family adults seem to know all the answers and have plenty of time for you. Maybe your older brother gives you some good advice. Or you all might have a good laugh together watching old home movies. These times makes families close and strong.

Of course, there are other times when things aren't going so great. Maybe your mom comes home from work tired and doesn't feel up to helping you with your math homework. Or your dad might be struggling with a big financial problem and can't find time to play ball with you. Parents have a lot to worry about. Sometimes you just have to cut them some slack.

How? One way is to reach out during difficult or busy times. Ask your mom or dad what's going on and what you can do to help. Offer to do the laundry or take your sister to the park so your folks can get other things done. Being part of a family is a two-way deal. Your parents love and support you—you can do your best to help them, too.

COMMUNICATION IS IMPORTANT

"Why can't I go outside on my own or bike on a busy road? I'm not four years old."
—Lance, 12

"I'm tired of hearing maybes. I want strong, clear answers (yes or no)."
—Kevin, 13

"That's not fair!" are words you might find yourself saying at home. Maybe your dad or mom wants you to go to bed when you want to stay up to watch TV or play on the computer. Or perhaps your dad tells you to spend more time practicing your instrument or doing homework. Rules might be a problem, too. It might seem like your older sister can do whatever she wants, but you don't have the same privileges. Parents usually have good intentions. They're trying to keep their kids healthy and safe. When they don't want you to do something, they probably have what they think are good reasons for it.

If you think parents are being unfair, sit down and have a calm conversation about it. It can be helpful to think about what you want to say before you sit down together. Give your side of things and offer solutions for fixing the problem. You can start off with, "Mom, can we talk about my bedtime?" or, "Dad, I have some ideas about raising my allowance." When you show them respect, parents are more likely to listen to what you have to say. You might even change their minds.

TIPS FOR TALKING TO PARENTS

1. Pick a time when you know parents are not busy and can talk.

2. Stay cool. Talking calmly will make parents more likely to hear you out.

3. Don't blame. Instead talk about how you're feeling.

4. Know what you want to say. Write it out first, if it helps.

5. Offer suggestions for solving the problem or getting what you want.

6. Listen to their side and be willing to compromise.

The Lowdown

HOT TOPICS IN THE HOME

Has this ever happened to you? You're watching your favorite TV show and your dad comes by and turns off the tube. "Hey . . . ," you start to say, but your dad interrupts, "After your homework's done." You look at the books in your lap and say, "But I'm doing my homework now." Your dad just crosses his arms and gives you his "do-your-homework" look.

Homework is one of the big things guys and parents often argue about. But it doesn't have to be. Saying that you'll do it later doesn't usually satisfy most parents. Instead, work out a schedule for getting your schoolwork done. If there's something you want to do at night, plan to get work done right after school. Your dad or mom probably won't care when you do your homework—as long as it isn't late at night. They just want you to set aside a time to get it done.

Often the homework debate is related to computer or TV time. Parents might think you spend too many hours in front of a screen. You'll have to talk with them about how much they think is too much. And games and television programs can create other problems, too. Your mom or dad might worry about what you see on Web sites, on TV, and in games. Find out what they're comfortable with and what they think you're ready for.

FACT: Video games aren't real—but they can seem real. Experts have learned that violent games can increase anger and aggression in a teen's brain. This doesn't mean you'll turn into a brute just because you play a violent video game, but a heavy diet of video violence can do some damage over time. Killing and fighting can start to seem normal. They're not!

FRIENDS AND FAMILY CAN MIX

"I wish my parents would notice the responsibility and maturity I show."
—Ron, 12

Can I stay at Tyler's until 8:30 if I call back at 8:00 to check in?

Family rules can cause big problems when it comes to friends. Your parents might not care when you tell them that your buddy has a lot more freedom than you do. "We're not his parents," they might say. "We are yours and this is the way we do things." You might wish you could stay out as late or do as many things as your pals. But remember that what works for one family often doesn't for another.

More serious family clashes can happen when your dad or mom believe friends are bad influences. Maybe they act, dress, or think in ways your folks don't agree with. This not only causes problems at home, but can also hurt friendships. What can you do? Listen to and respect what your parents are saying. But stand up for friends if you feel your mom and dad aren't being fair to them. Try to include friends in family activities. Parents might change their minds about someone when they know the person better.

With rules and friends, talk with parents about how you feel and try to come up with solutions that work for everyone (maybe using tips from page 49). They just might start giving you more chances to earn their trust. Family life works best when it's give and take.

WAYS FOR FAMILIES TO GET CLOSER

Getting closer to your family can start with some simple steps that you can be the first to take. Try these ideas for spending time together.

1. Eat meals together. It seems simple, but can make a big difference. If dinner doesn't work because of busy schedules, try breakfast.

2. Take a walk, play catch, or ride bikes together.

3. Ask family members about how their day was. Talk about your own activities at school.

4. Work on projects together. Help your mom fix the faucet. Work in the garden with your dad.

5. Go places together. Head to the park, a local sports event, the movies, or a museum.

6. Be nice to each other. Tell your parents you love them. Say, "Way to go!" when your brother brings home a good grade. Let your sister know that she's great at soccer.

YOU CAN HELP YOUR FAMILY

If your mom sticks another "To Do" list in your notebook, you'll go nuts, right? You've got enough on your mind—school, tests, making the team, a problem with a friend. Who wants to worry about mowing the lawn or vacuuming the rug after school?

When I was a kid, I didn't like some chores either. I had to do the usual things, like help clean the kitchen or take out the garbage. But I also had the job of watching my younger brother when my mom was at work. I thought my brother was a pain. He often didn't listen to me or help around the house, like he was supposed to. Sometimes, I thought it was unfair to me.

But if you think about it, everyone in a family has responsibilities, or certain things they have to do. Your mom and dad probably have to work to support the family. The shopping, cleaning, and home repairs need to be done. Working together—with everyone contributing—helps families survive and thrive.

Instead of thinking about how to get out of your chores, find ways to get them done quickly. The faster you finish them up, the more time you'll have for friends and your interests. And your parents will probably appreciate it when you pitch in without complaints or without being asked. When everybody contributes, families get along better.

MONEY ISN'T EVERYTHING

No matter how hard parents work, many families often go through tough times with money. You may know this firsthand. Families can get behind on the bills. Parents can lose a job or have their hours cut. If these things happen in your family, it might seem like the only word you hear is "no." (As in, "No, we can't afford that.") It can be hard to look around and see kids wearing the newest sneakers or playing the latest video game, knowing you don't have the same things.

When money is tight, adults at home might get stressed. I once lost my job, and I worried about how I would support my family. I sat down with my wife and daughter to tell them that we would get through this hard time, that I would find a new job, but that we would need to be more careful with money. We knew that if we pulled together as a family, everything would turn out okay. And it did. Within a couple of months, I found a new job—one even better than the one I had lost. My wife found work, too. And my daughter learned to appreciate what we did have. She realized that things she once saw as important—new clothes or trips—didn't mean as much as she thought.

We survived by pulling together and trying to do our best. And we learned that the most important things are not things you can buy, but the people you love.

A GUY LIKE YOU

When **ALBERT PUJOLS** comes to the plate, major league pitchers get nervous. The St. Louis Cardinals star has power to both fields and a high batting average—something many home-run hitters lack. That's not the only thing that sets Albert apart from the average major leaguer. For one, he grew up in very difficult circumstances in the Dominican Republic, an island country in the Caribbean Sea. With 12 children, Albert's family stayed at a government camp for people living in poverty. That didn't stop him from growing up with an optimistic attitude. His family, especially his grandmother, gave him the love and support he needed—something he values highly to this day. Says Albert, "What motivates me more than money are God and my family."

48

DIVORCE ISN'T YOUR FAULT

Big events can really shake up a family, leaving you feeling as if you're not on solid ground. I was 14 when my parents got divorced. They had been unhappy together for many years, but for me the divorce had the effect of an earthquake. I worried it was my fault—that I hadn't said the right words to keep them together. I even remember crying and begging my father on the phone one night to return home after he left my mother. He did return, but not for long. "Didn't they love my brother and me enough to stay together?" I asked myself.

Over time, I realized that the divorce was *not* my fault—that no matter how much I loved my parents, I didn't have the power to keep them together. I also learned that divorce changes a family, but it doesn't destroy it. It takes time to adjust to new living arrangements, including the possibility of stepparents and stepsiblings. You might not see one of your parents as often as you'd like. But you can still stay in touch through visits, phone calls, email, and letters. Just because parents aren't around as much doesn't mean they stop loving you—or that you'll stop loving them.

Divorce creates feelings that can be hard to handle. I was angry with my parents for making my world change so much. It took a long time for me to work through those strong feelings. It didn't help that divorce was considered shameful to talk about in those days. Today things are different, and families going though a divorce can see a counselor or therapist. Many adults realize that talking about feelings can help you understand them better.

Take Action!

Make a list of people you can talk to if your family ever goes through tough times. The list can include relatives, adults at school, a religious leader, a youth group leader, or some of your friends. Be sure to include each person's telephone number and email address. Keep the list handy so you never have to put off getting in touch with someone when you're ready to talk.

CHECK THIS OUT

How to Survive Your Parents' Divorce by Gayle Kimball. Thoughts from over 250 young people on how to deal with divorce. Real-life advice for all kinds of family situations.

49
The Lowdown

NEW FAMILY SITUATIONS

Not long after my parents divorced, my mother remarried. Suddenly, I had a stepfather. At first I resented him. I wanted my real father back, even if he and my mom didn't get along. And I didn't want a stranger coming into our home trying to be my dad, setting different rules, and telling me what to do.

If you have a stepmother or stepfather, you might feel the same way. Or maybe the parent you live with is starting a new relationship and you're worried about what might happen next. It's hard for anyone to accept a new person into the family. You might still wish for your mom or dad to come back. You probably still have a lot of love and loyalty for them, even if they don't live with you. There might be times in your new family situation when you're angry or upset and have to work things out with your mom or dad and the new adult on the scene. It might help to know that it's not easy for them either. Put yourself in their shoes. They're trying to get used to the change, too.

BARACK OBAMA understands what it's like to go through a lot of family changes. The fifth African American elected to the U.S. Senate, Obama is also a graduate of Harvard Law School, a former civil rights lawyer, and a best-selling author.

Obama's parents met and married in Hawaii. His father, who was from Kenya, left the family when Obama was two to study at Harvard and eventually return to his native country. Obama spent his early years in the home his mother and grandparents shared. Things changed again when he was six. His mother remarried and the family moved to Indonesia, where Obama's stepfather helped provide him with a loving home. After three years in Indonesia, Obama moved back to Hawaii to live with his grandparents.

Obama met his father only once—when he was ten years old. Despite moving around a lot and being part of a shifting family, Obama considers his childhood a happy one. He credits all of the many members of his family—his father, mother, stepfather, grandparents, and other relatives—for shaping his outlook on life and the values he carries today to his service in the senate.

MAKE THE BEST OF A MOVE

New family situations often mean you'll be moving from one place to another. But divorce and separation aren't the only reasons families move. A parent might get a new job in another state. Or, maybe rent goes up in the building and the family has to move to another part of the city.

One thing is definite: moving means there will be a change in your world. There was in mine when my parents divorced and my mother moved my brother and me to a new neighborhood. For me, moving meant giving up the life I had known—my old neighborhood, my friends, the closeness to relatives I liked to visit. I had to change schools and find new friends—a challenge for anyone.

Moving is a big deal, but good can come from it. With each move my family made, I had the chance to do positive things for myself. I made a decision to overcome shyness and make more friends. I learned to use the energy from anxious feelings to work harder in school and get better grades. After one move, I became a reporter for the school newspaper. The other students who worked on the paper became a second family to me—something I would have missed if I hadn't gone to that school and tried something new. Not only that, the experience helped shape who I was and who I became. I later got a job as a reporter and have worked for newspapers all my life.

TIPS FOR MOVING

BEFORE YOU MOVE:

1. Keep a journal. Write down memories and feelings you have about your old neighborhood. Paste pictures in the journal.

2. Say goodbye to your friends. Make plans to hang out with the old pals one last time—or have them all over for a farewell party. Tell them you want to stay in contact and exchange addresses. Email is also a great way to stay in touch.

3. Learn about your new neighborhood. Go online to find information on places to visit, youth groups, and other activities that are available in the place you're moving to. (You can do this for free at the library.)

4. Get information about your new school. Most schools have a Web site where you can learn about clubs, teams, teachers, and classes. (You can also call.)

AFTER YOU MOVE:

1. Explore your new neighborhood. Visit in person places you found online.

2. Join activities. Find fun things to do at school, after school, and in your new community. This can help you make new friends.

3. Keep in touch with old friends. Call or email and tell them about your new neighborhood. There's no reason why they can't remain your friends for life.

4. Keep up with your journal. Write about how your new home, friends, and neighborhood are different.

THERE'S LIFE AFTER LOSS

> "My grandpa is sick and I'm afraid he's going to die."
> —Reuben, 10

Many guys who took my survey mentioned worrying about the death of family members. Losing someone you love is one of hardest things in life. I know from personal experience. Both my grandmother and father died when I was young. Their deaths hit me hard. I thought they had deserted me when I needed them. I wasn't prepared to deal with strong feelings that came with loss—like fear, and sadness, and anger.

You might want to close yourself up and not talk about it—like I did at first. But adults in your life want to help. They know that the best way to work through hard feelings is to talk about them. Sharing with a parent, teacher, or counselor is the first step toward getting through. And just like I had to, you'll learn to continue with your life as best as you can.

A comforting thought is that people we lose stay with us forever in other ways. We keep their memory alive through our own actions. I remember my dad each day—especially his kindness and gentleness—and honor him by trying to live by his example. And every time I welcome someone warmly into my home I pay respect to my grandmother, who was such a friendly, fun-loving person.

WAYS TO KEEP ALIVE THE MEMORY OF A LOVED ONE

1. Talk with your family about the person you lost. Remember and laugh about the things he or she did. Come up with traditions to honor them.

2. Write a letter to the loved one. Explain what the person meant to you. Keep your loved one's photograph near your letter.

3. Take up a hobby or activity that reminds you of the person you lost.

4. Plant some bulbs in the person's memory that will bloom each spring.

5. Keep a collection of things that you and the person shared together.

6. Do a good deed in the person's name. If the person died from a disease, you might join in a money-raising activity—like a walkathon—for a charity that is working to find a cure.

52

OLDER FAMILY MEMBERS CAN SHARE THEIR WISDOM

After the terrorist attacks on September 11, 2001, and the start of the wars in both Afghanistan and Iraq, I reached out to the young people who read my newspaper pages. I encouraged them to talk with an older person they know who has lived through war or troubled times and has lost loved ones. My hope was for readers to learn that each generation experiences its own hard times and challenges—but that each generation (including yours) also finds strength and the courage to survive.

By talking to older members of your family—grandparents, great grandparents, great aunts or uncles—you discover their wisdom. If you don't have older relatives, talk to other trusted elders, such as people in your house of worship. Ask them about the struggles and challenges they faced as they grew up. Learn about how they carried on and kept hope alive in their heart. They may tell you that the most important things in life are having a loving family, good health, friendships, courage, belief in God, and the strength to be happy with one another even when times are hard.

Ask your mom or dad about reaching out to an older relative, neighbor, or member of your religious community. This may be as simple as calling your grandfather on the phone or paying a visit to an elderly neighbor.

53 GUYS LOOK UP TO FAMILY MEMBERS

"My mom and dad are intelligent and kind. They're everything I want to become."
—Latrell, 10

"My dad is a very caring and loving person. He's also respected and successful because he has incredible drive and smarts."
—Will, 12

SURVEY SAYS...

"My role models are my brothers. They all went to college and have good jobs."
—Carson, 10

"My uncle Gilbert has respect for everybody and tries to help them."
—John, 11

"I have my mom as a role model because she is going to school and is very independent."
—Mike, 13

"My parents and grandparents are awesome guardians and taught me to see the glass half full."
—Rodney, 13

"My grandfather is my role model. He's weird and a lot of fun. We like a lot of the same things."
—P.J., 11

"My cousin worked really hard in high school and college and got a great job. He is a great person, too."
—Travis, 11

"I look up to my uncle because he's a lawyer and that's what I want to be."
—Jake, 12

"My dad seems to have done everything the right way in life."
—Tucker, 12

"My parents are very hard workers and out of that hard work came success."
—Brian, 13

"I respect my sister a lot because she is sensitive, funny, and understanding. She can help you with just about any problem."
—Jacques, 12

BEING PART OF A FAMILY CAN BE GREAT

"My family loves me and I love them back."
—Juwan, 12

"I always feel loved and encouraged by my mom and dad."
—Terry, 10

Family life can be filled with conflict at times. The next time you're annoyed or angry with your mom or dad, catch your breath and think for a moment about a fun time you had together. Was it a vacation to the beach or a lake? Was it when your mom helped you make a terrific costume for Halloween, or when your dad took you fishing? A time over the holiday season when you all participated in a family tradition? There can be lots of good moments in the life of a family.

I remember my happiest times as a boy were on Sunday afternoons when my father would take my mother, my brother, and me—along with my grandfather and aunts and uncles—to an Italian restaurant in our neighborhood called Mary's. We would eat great food and joke and laugh. I felt so loved and protected and didn't want Sunday to end. Memories of those Sundays kept me going even after my parents were divorced.

What can you do to make great family moments happen? Talk to your dad or mom about having a family night. Try one night each month—or more if you want—where everybody gets together to watch a video, go on a picnic, or play a game you all enjoy. My family had a special tradition an evening each week when every family member, including my grandparents, would sing or tell jokes. Your family can choose its own tradition—something fun and meaningful that will bring everyone closer together.

SCHOOL

55 SCHOOL IS YOUR FIRST CAREER

"Doing well in school is important to succeed. Every good job is looking for someone who is smart and gets good grades."
—Erik, 11

"I'm still getting used to the homework amounts."
—Brian, 13

Just like adolescence is a time for learning information you'll use later on, school also gives you a chance to practice things you will need as an adult. You might even want to consider school your first career. Think about it. You're learning a lot and developing new skills. And habits you get into now to stay on top of your work can carry over into how you do things in college or at a future job.

Many guys who took my survey talked about school in a positive way. But lots of others found it tough going. They mentioned some of the things that gave them problems: tests, speeches, projects, reports,

due dates, homework, complicated class schedules. These were only some of the issues that were mentioned. Bullies, cliques, and peer pressure also came up a lot. (For more on surviving the social scene at school, see page 79.)

But even guys who said they had trouble at school didn't forget about the good things they did there. They were excited to learn new information, spend time with friends, play sports, join student groups, and meet teachers and coaches who could act as mentors. Most found ways to follow their own interests and make school a place where they could work toward goals.

CHECK THESE OUT

It's My Life—School (www.pbskids.org/ itsmylife/school). Find advice on dealing with all kinds of issues that come up when you start middle school or junior high.

Too Old for This, Too Young for That! by Harriet S. Mosatche and Karen Unger. The lowdown on the middle school years. Includes tips on homework, tests, teachers, friends, family, and more.

61

A GUY LIKE YOU

MICHAEL CRICHTON is the best-selling author of many books that have been made into movies. Before *Jurassic Park*, *The Lost World*, and *Twister* lit up the screen, they were books that thrilled readers and sold millions of copies. Michael's career aspirations may have begun in third grade. His class was assigned to write a skit to act out with puppets. Instead, Michael wrote a nine-page play! His reputation as a writer grew in middle school. Michael enjoyed writing so much he wrote extra papers for teachers—even though they did not ask for them. All of that time put into writing has paid off. Nearly every new book Michael Crichton publishes makes the best-seller list.

The Lowdown 56

LIFE IN MIDDLE SCHOOL

I remember the day I went to orientation for junior high school. Everyone there seemed so much older and more confident than me. I came home feeling like such a kid, and wondered how I would ever get used to the new school. In elementary school I was with the same class all day. In my new school I had to go on my own to different classes with different teachers and students. I had a lot more freedom, but also a lot more things to keep track of—schedules, subjects, homework, a locker, assignments, armloads of books.

It's natural to feel stressed out when you move to middle school or junior high. There are big changes in how things work. You have lots of new responsibilities but no single teacher to help you along as you learn the ropes. This is part of the plan. Middle school (or junior high) prepares you for high school, which then prepares you for college, technical school, or other training before you enter the full-time world of work. You become more and more independent as you move along.

The good news is that there is help when you need it. You just have to reach out and ask for it. Part of doing well in school is knowing what to do when you feel overwhelmed. Creating your own "support network"—teachers, guidance counselors, parents, older kids, and others who can help—can let you do that. Creating a support network is also a good idea when you move on to high school and college or other training you might do. When you surround yourself with people who can help, you'll be in a good position to handle any challenges that come up.

SCHOOL CAN BE TOUGH GOING

"When I started junior high I knew absolutely no one."
—Joe, 13

"I forget to do homework sometimes."
—Rog, 12

SURVEY SAYS...

"My school is really big on the popularity thing. There are different groups and where you hang out classifies who you are. It's pretty lame. I can't wait till high school."
—Julio, 12

"Things go wrong at school all the time. If you don't do this, you're stupid. If you do that, you're stupid. If you aren't smart your parents yell at you. If you are, you have no friends."
—Jack, 13

"Bullying happens a lot. Some kids don't have many friends and they get put down."
—Reg, 9

"Sometimes when I'm giving an oral presentation at school, I'm not confident and I mumble."
—Jon, 11

"I'm in all high classes and need a way to deal with the stress."
—Sherm, 12

"I get in trouble for socializing when I'm not supposed to."
—T.J., 11

"I try to take notes and follow along, but it doesn't work for me."
—Nigel, 12

"Things aren't explained very well."
—Frank, 12

"I have a hard time getting up so early."
—Mark, 11

"I don't like the bullies and cliques because they hurt people and make them feel left out."
—Santana, 12

"I don't get very good grades and my mom puts a lot of pressure on me, so school is very frustrating."
—Rich, 10

"My teachers don't understand me."
—Steve, 11

"I get bad grades."
—Cal, 11

"Memorizing 12 subjects is impossible. Especially if you forget your planner."
—Sam, 14

64

I know you're upset, but I think it's gonna be okay.

I just got out of algebra – half the class failed that test.

Mr. Jackson's talking about a re-test and offering extra points to anyone who wants to do some worksheets for practice.

You'll probably find out about it tomorrow.

Where does THAT get me?! I still don't understand this kind of math.

Hey, I did all right on my test. Maybe we can review over the weekend. You can stay over – I'm sure my mom'll be cool with it.

Yeah?

Okay, it's a go! Thanks, Jake!

Don't sweat it. I didn't get the stuff until I started going to a tutor on Tuesdays. I set it up with Mr. Jackson. Maybe you can come along next time.

That sounds great. Right now I can use all the help I can get.

Need some help in school? Read on for tips to bring your "A game" to the classroom.

65

TEACHERS WANT YOU TO SUCCEED

"Ms. Johnson, my science teacher, cares a lot for us. She's helped me do well in school."
—J.R., 13

I had a rough time learning how to read. It wasn't until a teacher gave me extra help after school that I was able to finally "get it." Her close, unselfish attention turned me around and gave me confidence. I discovered that with hard work and patience, I could learn almost anything I wanted to.

Think about the teachers in your life. There are probably some who have been a lot of help when you didn't understand something. Maybe there are others you have a hard time getting along with. It's easy to forget that teachers are people, too. Just like everybody else, they have bad days, get tired or cranky, and make mistakes. When you think teachers are giving you a hard time, meet them halfway. Talk with them about issues that come up—whether related to your grades, homework load, or how they treat you. Most teachers care about you and want to see you succeed. It's up to you to give a full effort.

TIPS FOR TALKING TO TEACHERS

1. Ask your teacher about a good time to talk. Blurting out problems in the middle of class isn't going to help—you'll only annoy your teacher or disrupt the class. See if you can meet before or after school, or during lunch break.

2. If you're feeling overwhelmed with homework, ask if you can break assignments into smaller pieces that work for both you and the teacher. If tests are the problem, ask for study tips.

3. If you feel that you're being unfairly singled out or criticized, talk honestly about how you feel. Try to understand your teacher's expectations and ask what you can do to meet them.

4. Keep the conversation positive. Talk about some of the good things you're getting from your class. When teachers feel appreciated, they're more willing to hear you out.

5. If there's a problem that you and a teacher just can't seem to work out, talk to adults at home. Together, look for solutions to make things better for you at school.

59

YOU CAN GET ORGANIZED

When it comes to getting organized for school, you might want to think of yourself as an executive. Executives watch over different parts of a company. They have to be organized and know how to manage their time. In my work as a manager at a newspaper, people relied on me to get a lot of things done. Before I started work each morning, I would think about the goals for that day and make a plan for doing everything. Like anyone, I also wanted to do some things just for myself—like spending time with my family, jogging, and playing music. Setting goals and managing my time allowed me to do that.

You can be an executive at school, too. Instead of a company, the things you watch over are you and your work. Your job is to keep track of assignments, books, and folders. You also need to juggle the time you spend on homework, sports, clubs, and family responsibilities. Organizing your time and materials isn't always easy, but it's the first step toward doing well. After all, you can't get points for an assignment that's lost on your bedroom floor. And not showing up—for class, afterschool activities, or for things going on at home—won't impress teachers, coaches, or parents. It will just get you in trouble.

Setting goals each day for what you need to do is a good place to start. And keeping a planner or schedule can help you stay on top of responsibilities. Learning to be organized and manage your time now will put you a step ahead to meet new challenges in school and later in the world of work.

TIPS FOR GETTING ORGANIZED

ORGANIZE YOUR THINGS

1. Clearly label all of your folders and notebooks for each class. Keep homework assignments in one place where you'll always know to find them.

2. Clean out your locker and backpack once a week so that you can throw out the things you don't need. Having too much junk lying around will make it easier to lose important papers like notes and assignments.

3. Have a study space at home where you can easily find references and supplies. Clean up your work area once a week so you can find everything you need.

ORGANIZE YOUR TIME

1. Use a planner or an assignment book to keep track of assignment due dates, tests, study times, and afterschool activities.

2. Look at your planner often and make a "To Do" list for each day. Cross items off when you finish them.

3. Set a specific time for doing certain activities. For example, plan to do your homework from 7:00 to 8:00 every night.

YOU CAN SURVIVE TEST STRESS

> "Cheating is not a good thing, but it is everywhere. It hurts you because you don't learn what you need to. Then you start to depend on the person you are cheating from."
> —Ricardo, 13

Sometimes the pressure to succeed at school can lead you to do something you'll later regret—cheat. When a bad grade is staring guys in the face, it's tempting for them to look for shortcuts to do well in classes. Some people decide it's okay to look at someone else's test—or to copy someone's assignment when a deadline gets close. Many times students can get away with stealing someone's answers or ace a test they didn't study for.

But cheating doesn't help—it only leads to failure. I learned the hard way when I cheated once on a test to get a better grade. Not getting the material the first time around caused problems for me later on. As the work got harder, I fell behind and didn't know what I was doing in the class. I also felt bad about what I'd done—I saw that I had cheated *myself.* By giving up when things got tough, I lost confidence in my ability to learn. I realized then that to feel good about myself and really succeed at school, I'd have to put in the time it took to understand the material and ask for help when I needed it.

TEST-TAKING TIPS

BEFORE THE TEST

1. Make sure you plan for enough time to study. Preparation is the #1 way to do well.

2. Ask your teacher what topic areas are most important to study. You might get some hints for what's on the test.

3. Make sure you get enough sleep the night before the test. On test day, have a good breakfast or lunch. And use the bathroom right before the test. Keeping your body happy will help you to concentrate.

4. Show up early for the test. Remember to bring all of the materials you'll need to take the test (extra pens and pencils or a calculator, for example).

DURING THE TEST

1. Keep a good attitude. If you start to feel nervous, take a few deep breaths to relax. Think, "I can do this."

2. Do the easiest problems first. Don't stay stuck on problems that are hard. If you have time, go back to them at the end.

3. Take your time. Rushing through a test can cause you to make careless mistakes.

4. If there's time, look over your test before you hand it in. (You might have missed a question.) But don't change any of your answers unless you are sure about them. Most times the first answer you pick is right.

GET THE HELP YOU NEED

I had a lot of trouble with math in school for a long time. I finally asked an older student who lived nearby to help me out. This took some courage—I was embarrassed to admit I was having problems. But it was the right thing to do. The girl was a good student and she worked with me day after day until math started to click for me. Asking for her help was my first step toward doing better in class.

If you're having a problem at school, the best thing to do is to talk to someone about it. Maybe a teacher will offer to stay with you after school or help you find a tutor. Someone in your family or neighborhood might be able to help. Ask around. The point is that you have to do something about the problem. Just complaining or worrying about a situation at school won't make it go away. Instead, work to find a solution.

CHECK THESE OUT

B.J. Pinchbeck's Homework Helper (school.discovery.com/homeworkhelp/bjpinchbeck). This Web site has over 700 links to helpful resources for English, math, science, social studies, and many other subjects.

Encarta Homework (encarta.msn.com/encnet/departments/homework). Homework tools for all of the main subjects in school. Features references (like atlases, encyclopedias, and dictionaries) for taking on projects and reports.

A GUY LIKE YOU

COLIN POWELL is widely respected for his government and military service. He has served under six presidents—including as secretary of state in George W. Bush's administration. In 35 years as a professional soldier, Powell achieved the rank of four-star General (the highest rank in the military) and held many important posts, like national security advisor and chairman of the Joint Chiefs of Staff. Growing up as the son of Jamaican immigrants in New York City, Powell had little idea of the greatness that awaited him. He admits to being an average student who had a hard time getting motivated for school. But with the encouragement of his parents, Powell worked hard and received a good education. Teachers also played a big role in his success, something he hasn't forgotten to this day. Powell remembers one teacher in particular—Miss Ryan, his English teacher: "I remember her because she was a hard teacher. She didn't let us get away with anything in class. She was determined that we would learn to use the English language properly. We also knew that she really liked us. And that's why she was so hard on us—because she wanted us to do well."

The Lowdown

GUYS IN SCHOOL

"Girls are treated better than guys."
—Quentin, 13

"Teachers think guys are troublemakers and girls are perfect. They make comments sometimes that I think are offensive to males."
—Eddie, 12

Does it ever seem like guys get a bad rap in school? Many who took my survey thought so. A lot of guys said that teachers treated girls better, and that it was always the guys who got in trouble. While it's not fair to teachers to say they favor girls, there are some reasons why guys' behavior sometimes stands out.

Part of the problem is that middle school guys are often naturally more active than the girls. You and your pals may have a lot of energy and have trouble sitting still. Testosterone—the main hormone causing changes in your body and mind—surges through you and can make you want to move or act out. It can take a lot of control to stay seated and not blurt things out. It's pretty easy for teachers to single guys out when it's more often them who are goofing off during class.

Your body *will* settle down over time and you won't have to pay as much attention to just sitting still. Until then, it's up to you to work hard to stay in charge of your actions. If behavior is a problem for you, talk with teachers and parents about ways they might help.

FACT: Guys are three times more likely to be diagnosed with ADHD (Attention-Deficit/Hyperactivity Disorder) than girls. People with ADHD have brains that work differently from most people. ADHD makes it hard to sit still or focus. It also can be hard to listen, stay quiet, or follow instructions. For guys who have ADHD, their behavior often upsets teachers, disrupts class, and gets in the way of learning. Sometimes they have to find different arrangements at school—like working in another classroom where they can get extra help.

A GUY LIKE YOU

Readers of all ages love the *Captain Underpants* books by **DAV PILKEY**. Dav wasn't what you would call a teacher's pet. Diagnosed with ADHD at a young age, Dav spent a lot of time out in the hallway. His teacher would send him there for making funny noises and disturbing the class. Dav was in the hall so often that he even had a desk there. He filled it with art supplies and drew pictures when his behavior took him from the class. He started to make up stories and create characters, too—including Captain Underpants. Even though he had a lot of trouble because of ADHD, Dav stuck out school and was able to finish. Today, Dav is an award-winning author and illustrator whose books are popular with millions of kids.

63 OTHER GUYS ARE THINKING ABOUT BEHAVIOR

"Sometimes my medicine for ADHD doesn't work and I go crazy."
—Will, 12

"I get in trouble sometimes. Usually I'm doing something stupid at school."
—Dominic, 10

SURVEY SAYS...

"I get discipline slips a lot."
—Royce, 12

"Okay, I never stop talking. But I get blamed for other stuff I don't even do."
—Michael, 10

"It seems like everything is a distraction for me at school. Sports, girls, and music. I can barely focus."
—Trevor, 11

"I normally get into trouble for blurting out or being impatient."
—Ricky, 12

"I try to stay out of trouble by following the rules, but it's hard at times."
—Stan, 13

"One time a teacher punished the whole class for something one person did. Everyone was appalled."
—Greg, 10

"Teachers favor girls. If a guy and girl are talking, the guy would get a detention while the girl gets nothing. It's so unfair!"
—Donyell, 13

"I have never had a teacher that is not somehow sexist against boys. They think guys don't try as hard as girls. Not true at all!"
—Isaac, 12

"A teacher once told me that boys have a history of being bad and girls don't. I don't think that is fair because some of us guys aren't bad and teachers just assume we are."
—Jeff, 13

EVERYONE CAN LEARN

> "The way I like to learn isn't by reading, but by having a teacher go over assignments and make sure that you understand it. My reading comprehension isn't good."
> —Jamie, 13

> "I went to a special school for a while to deal with my learning disability. I didn't want to, but my parents made me. The school really helped, and now I'm back in my old school. Looking back, I agree it was the best thing I could have done."
> —Craig, 12

Behavior isn't the only thing that causes guys grief at school. More guys than girls are diagnosed with learning differences (LD). You might know that everyone learns differently and at their own rate. Learning differences can make certain work harder to do. Some learning differences—like ADHD—can make it hard to concentrate on any kind of work. The important thing to remember is that you're not "stupid" if you have some problems at school. Everyone has learning strengths and weaknesses. The key is to get the help you need in the areas that are hard for you. Talk with your parents and teachers about the subjects that give you trouble and work together to figure out solutions for success.

One easy thing you can do is talk to teachers about different ways to show what you know. Maybe you've memorized tons of facts about history, but you have trouble doing a report on them because you're still developing your writing skills. Why not ask if you can do an oral report instead? You'll still have to practice writing, but at least you can show what you know in history. Making these kinds of agreements may not always be possible, but teachers may have other ideas for helping you out.

Learning differences can make things hard in school. But if you don't give up and try your best, you'll come out a winner.

CHECK THESE OUT

The Survival Guide for Kids with LD by Gary Fisher and Rhoda Cummings. This book has lots of information on all of the different kinds of learning differences. You'll find tips for dealing at school, handling hard issues at home, and getting along with other kids.

LD OnLine Kidzone (www.ldonline.org/kidzone). Featuring information on learning disabilities, success strategies, and the stories and artwork of real kids with learning differences, this is a nice site for learning and having some fun. Plus you can share your own stories or artwork.

65

EVERYONE HAS LEARNING STRENGTHS

There are lots of different ways to be smart. And tests and assignments aren't always the best ways to prove it. Howard Gardner is a psychologist who has found eight different ways that people learn and show their abilities. He calls the eight ways *multiple intelligences*.

1. **LINGUISTIC INTELLIGENCE:** You're good with words, including reading, writing, and speaking.

2. **MUSICAL INTELLIGENCE:** You like music and can hear patterns in it.

3. **LOGICAL-MATHEMATICAL INTELLIGENCE:** Figuring out problems with numbers and math rules comes naturally to you.

4. **SPATIAL INTELLIGENCE:** You might be good at art, working with pictures, and other projects where you need to see things in new ways.

5. **BODILY-KINESTHETIC INTELLIGENCE:** Using your body in different ways is often easy, including in sports, dancing, or acting.

6. **INTERPERSONAL INTELLIGENCE:** You get along well with others and understand what they are thinking and feeling.

7. **INTRAPERSONAL INTELLIGENCE:** You understand your own emotions and know how to express what you are thinking and feeling.

8. **NATURALIST INTELLIGENCE:** You like outdoor stuff, including plants and animals, and you enjoy collecting and classifying things.

Everybody has all eight of these, but for each person some intelligences are a lot stronger than others. The thing to remember is that you have unique gifts and talents—including some that might not show up in the work you do for school. You can still do well in any subject; sometimes all you have to do is put in a little more effort—or get some help—to stay on track.

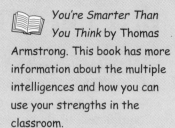

CHECK THIS OUT

You're Smarter Than You Think by Thomas Armstrong. This book has more information about the multiple intelligences and how you can use your strengths in the classroom.

How are you smart? Think or write about the kinds of things you like and do well.

WORKING TOGETHER HELPS GET THINGS DONE

You've probably heard the expression "No man can move a mountain." It means that it can sometimes be too hard for one person to complete a really huge job alone. Now's a good time to remember this. In middle school, you have to work on projects in groups more often than ever before. Part of your grade will depend on how well you work with others and share responsibilities.

Of course, teamwork isn't only helpful on science projects or history assignments. Sports, student government, and other extracurricular activities are all places you need to cooperate with others. Can you imagine, for example, taking the baseball field on your own? You'd have to pitch and field balls for every position. (That's a lot of running around!) In baseball, like most things, you need teamwork. Learning to get along and work with others now will set you up for the future, too, as you'll need these skills on any job you decide to do.

Take Action!

Think about a time when you worked together with someone to accomplish a big task. Is there another "mountain" you want to move? Who can help you out? What can you do to start?

TIGER WOODS has earned a lot of respect and admiration worldwide for his play on the golf course. Of his many accomplishments, he won six professional major championships and three U.S. Amateur championships through age 25. As a boy, Tiger was so eager to play the game that he would call his dad at work and beg him to take him out to the course. While Earl and Kutilda Woods encouraged their son's childhood dream to become a professional golfer, there was one thing that came before the game: school.

Tiger's parents had a rule that he had to finish his homework before he could practice. His studying paid off—Tiger earned excellent grades. All these years and tournament wins later, his parents' lesson has not been lost on Tiger. In 1996, he worked with his dad to create the Tiger Woods Foundation—a charity that supports youth education programs. Tiger considers his work for the foundation more important than winning tournaments. He says: "I was very fortunate to have teachers in my life that took the time to help me, and I want to build something that will give kids the same opportunity."

YOU WIN WHEN YOU GIVE YOUR ALL

67

If you ask people who are successful what's most important for doing well in life, many will say hard work. Giving 100 percent of yourself when you're doing something that is hard or new is a big step toward achieving great things.

I was a slow learner in school. When things didn't come easily for me, I had to make myself study and study until I finally understood the work. It was a good habit to get into. Throughout my life, I've used the same determination to succeed. I've been able to achieve a lot, including being a manager for a major newspaper. The key is to believe in your goals and to be willing to give everything you have to reach them. You might have to make sacrifices along the way—maybe you'll have less time to do some of the things you enjoy. But succeeding in school is one of the most important things you can do. The hard work you put in now will help you achieve all of the things you want to do later in life.

68 GUYS' THOUGHTS ON SUCCESS

> "I try to stay out of trouble by not goofing around."
> —Priest, 11

> "I don't have too many problems at school because when we're in class I focus on what we're doing."
> —Luke, 13

> "I put school before everything except my family."
> —Javier, 12

SURVEY SAYS...

"I get my homework done and that helps my grades."
—Samson, 12

"Last year I got B's and C's. This year I am a lot more organized and I am getting A's and B's."
—Roderick, 12

"I usually listen to directions and understand assignments. I'm nice, too, so I don't get in trouble."
—Lebron, 13

"I do good work and show my teachers that I put in effort."
—Ryan, 12

"I usually do well in school because I practice things before I have to do them on a test."
—Brad, 11

"I get good grades, but I have to force myself to do the work. It's extremely hard to sit in a chair for a long time, but I try to focus."
—Gary, 10

"I don't try to be the greatest at everything. I work hard and do my best, but I don't put pressure on myself."
—Richard, 13

SCHOOL CAN BE FUN

69

"I play in the school band. It's fun to go on trips and stuff."
—Dave, 12

"My favorite thing about school is that there are a lot of opportunities for extracurricular activities. I'm glad that there are many choices about what we can do."
—Henri, 13

It was while working on the school newspaper that I discovered my passion for writing and journalism. My experience there turned out to be a stepping stone for the work I decided to do as an adult. There are a lot of great opportunities—or stepping stones—for you, too. School is a place where you can follow many interests outside of the classroom. Extracurricular activities let you learn new things and develop your skills. Not only that, joining teams and clubs are good ways to make friends and feel more "at home" in school. Sports, drama, the school newspaper, band, science or math clubs, student government—you have a wide variety of options to pick from. Try something new. Who knows what will happen?

VOTE JAKE FOR STUDENT COUNCIL

Take Action!

Think about one new activity you're interested in trying. Is there a team or club you can join at school? Set a goal to get involved, and go for it!

70

THE FUTURE BEGINS NOW

Think about this for a minute: when you look around at the students in your class, you're looking at something of the future. There's the guy who always seems to be a leader. When he gets older he might be an executive in a big company. The math or science whiz might become an economist or biologist and change the way people think about the world. There's the girl with incredible smarts who may one day become a lawyer and argue cases before the U.S. Supreme Court.

What's your place? Where do you want to go? Thinking about this now can make school a lot more interesting and fun. You can put lessons from the classroom to work toward your future—whatever you might want that to be.

Take Action!

Think about what you'd like to do as an adult. Are there classes or activities you can take now to learn more about that career? Write down your goals and things that you might do at school to reach them.

RELATIONSHIPS

The Lowdown

SOCIAL LIFE IN MIDDLE SCHOOL

"With some groups of kids, you have to be someone else to fit in."
—Alex, 12

"I fit in with other kids at school, but I'm not sure why. I can be myself, but I sort of wonder who that is. Class clown? Athletic? Geek? I don't know."
—Ollie, 11

These days you may be spending more time with friends—and less with family—than you used to. You might be in more activities at school, and you probably share interests with people outside of school, too—like skateboarding, playing music together, or other fun things. Maybe you've noticed that some relationships are a lot stronger than before. Some of the buddies you have now could remain friends for your entire life.

Stronger friendships and more independence are nice perks of getting older. But some other parts of social life during adolescence can be hard to figure out. Many guys from my survey talked about tough situations that come up during the middle school years—including dealing with cliques, bullies, and peer pressure. With lots of new faces and groups, some guys worried a lot about where they fit in.

Relationships with girls also had guys asking questions. Many were taking a stronger interest in girls—as friends and sometimes more. Handling situations with them was something many guys wanted to learn more about.

CHECK THESE OUT

 The How Rude!™ Handbook of Friendship & Dating Manners for Teens by Alex J. Packer. Useful (and funny!) advice for all kinds of social situations.

It's My Life—Friends (www.pbskids.org/ itsmylife/friends). A Web site with advice, games, and other useful features for getting the scoop on social life.

GUYS' THOUGHTS ON THE SOCIAL SCENE

"I always fit in with my group of friends, but sometimes I wander off to other groups and I don't know what to say."
—Malcolm, 13

"When you're younger, you change who you are around people. When you get older, you act the way you are and decide who your friends are."
—Noah, 11

SURVEY SAYS...

"I don't have too many friends, and people call me 'Goose.'"
—Joe, 12

"I have friends who think they know me, but they really don't."
—Hank, 11

"People make fun of me for not having a girlfriend."
—Jorgé, 13

"I usually fit in with other kids because we all like the same stuff."
—Ben, 11

"Sometimes kids make fun of the way I dress."
—Matt, 12

"One of my friends was a year older than me. We hung out outside of school, but had different groups there. Eventually we stopped hanging out."
—Bert, 10

"I can talk to kids that are popular or not popular. They're all pretty much like me."
—Mewelde, 12

"I fit in with most people, but sometimes they think I am too smart and not their friend."
—Randy, 11

"I get into a lot of fights."
—Tavis, 10

"I don't talk a lot and have trouble fitting in with people."
—Jack, 12

"For some reason, lots of kids are against me."
—Charlie, 11

"A friend and I had some problems in fifth grade, but now we're friends again."
—Juan, 13

"There are some groups of kids I don't like and they don't like me."
—Allan, 11

IDEAS FOR MAKING FRIENDS

Making good friends is one of the best parts of getting older. But as guys in the survey said, this isn't always easy. Many mentioned that they had a hard time talking to new classmates or people they didn't know. Others felt like they were on the outside of groups and looking in.

It's natural to feel uncertain as you make your way through the social scene. It can seem like everyone else is a lot more confident and accepted. It might help to remember that even guys who seem very sure of themselves are often nervous about new social situations. Middle school is a big adjustment for everyone.

TIPS FOR MAKING FRIENDS

1. Take the first step by smiling at the person you'd like to meet and introducing yourself in a clear voice. ("Hi, my name's Ali. What's yours?")

2. Be friendly. Letting people know that you like spending time with them can make them enjoy spending time with you, too. ("That was a great game. We should play again sometime.")

3. Talk about interests you share. If you know someone likes a subject or activity that you also enjoy, bring it up in your conversation. ("You're in the band, aren't you? I play, too.")

4. Ask questions and listen closely to what a person says. Showing interest in someone and the things they care about can make them feel good. ("Camping sure sounds like a great time.")

5. Find positive things about new friends. Don't say things that you don't mean, but make other people see that you admire their qualities and achievements. ("That was a great answer you gave in class today.")

6. Join activities that you enjoy at school and in the community. It's hard to meet others if you spend all of your time alone in front of the TV or computer.

A GUY LIKE YOU

Money can't buy friendship, but a few laughs can sometimes open up doors. Just take the actor **JIM CARREY**. During his school years, Carrey used humor to make friends. Bringing out his impressions for classmates at recess made him a big hit on the playground. He could imitate nearly anyone—including the principal—and the laughs he got won him more friends than he ever had before. Jim's skills didn't only come in handy in the friend department. Being able to act out many zany characters brought Jim success with films like *Ace Ventura: Pet Detective*, *Dumb and Dumber*, and *The Mask*.

BE A GOOD FRIEND

"My friends and I stick up for one another. Even though we're not from the popular group, we don't let others put us down."
—Rob, 13

"I like having all kinds of friends because they can help you in life."
—Val, 12

"My friends are great. They accept and support me."
—Travis, 10

What can you do to be a good friend? You probably have some idea from the friendships you've had up till now. Qualities some guys talked about on the survey were loyalty, patience, and honesty. There's not any one secret to being a great friend. But there is a pretty good way to go about it: If you want friends, be a friend.

That means being kind and considerate. It means listening when a friend wants to talk about something that's bothering him, and supporting him as he tries to work through problems. Friends respect and listen to each other even when they disagree. They're sensitive, too. They don't brag about scoring 15 points in the first quarter when a buddy has had a bad game. And they definitely don't ditch out when things don't go right or someone more interesting or "cooler" comes along.

The great thing about friends is that they're going through many of the same things you are. You can learn a lot from one another—and sticking together will make you all stronger.

Take Action!

What makes a good friend? Write down some of the things you look for. How are you a friend to others?

FRIENDSHIPS HAVE ROCKY SPOTS

Middle school presents new pitfalls for friendships—especially when you and your friends start doing different activities. You might want to try out for the baseball team while a buddy joins the drama club. Practice schedules probably keep you both busy and you each might really like hanging out with people from your own activities. It can be hard to figure out a way to make your relationship work.

In some cases, you'll find the time to keep friendships going strong. In others, you might drift apart. That's okay. Just because you don't spend as much time together doesn't mean you can't still care about and have respect for each other.

Even with really good friends there'll be tough days when the two of you don't get along. Maybe you have different opinions about something. A friend might do something you don't like—or you'll do things that bother him. When you and a buddy have differences, don't fly off the handle. Instead, talk things out and listen to each other. Most issues, even big ones, aren't worth ending a friendship over.

TIPS FOR SMOOTHING OVER DIFFERENCES WITH FRIENDS

1. Think about what's bothering you. Practice what you want to say to a friend. (Talking to someone other than your friend first—a parent or teacher—can help.)

2. Talk with your friend about how you feel in a calm way. Don't blame.

3. Listen to what your friend has to say. Get his side of things. The whole problem may be one big misunderstanding.

4. Come up with a solution that you both can live with. Apologize to each other if you need to.

5. Think about the good things in your friendship. This can help put conflicts in perspective.

Welcome to American Guy!

We're here tonight to test the social smarts of Jake and Tyler.

YEAH! ALL RIGHT! CLAP CLAP

WOOHOO CLAP CLAP CLAP CLAP CLAP

Surviving the social scene is no easy task, and the guys will have their work cut out for them tonight.

Our judges will decide if Jake and Tyler have the respect it takes – for others and for themselves – to have a great social life.

Tyler's up first, let's see what he's got!

Can you tell me where the lab is?

Give the new kid a break!

Yeah, I know where the lab is – follow me.

That was a smooth recovery.

Ty hit a sour note when he and the group excluded the new kid. But helping out definitely showed he's got respect. He might have made a new friend, too.

Jake's up – will he stand up against his buddy's rude behavior?

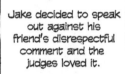

DO WHAT'S RIGHT FOR YOU

"I deal with peer pressure by just saying no. I say, 'I don't want to do that,' and usually my friends just leave me alone."
—Cory, 12

"If you're putting on a show to impress a person or group, you are not letting your true self come out."
—Mitchell, 11

In school, there is a lot of pressure to fit in. Wanting to fit in is fine—it's when others ask you to do things you don't want to do that problems can start. You might know guys (and girls) who pick on others, get in trouble with teachers, shoplift, or use cigarettes, alcohol, or other drugs. These are situations when you have to put fitting in into perspective. Is it really worth it to have these friends?

Part of getting older is learning to make good decisions. This includes choosing who you spend time with. Ask yourself, "Is this a person or group I really want to hang out with? Will the friendship help me be the person I want to be?" When a group doesn't respect what you want for *you*, it's time to look for other people who will. If the pressure is on, trust the voice inside that says what's right for you.

WAYS TO SAY NO AND STAY COOL

1. Suggest doing something else. "I don't want to do that. How 'bout we see a movie instead?"

2. Give a reason why you don't want to do something. "Sorry, but I don't want to hurt my body by smoking."

3. Change the subject. "I don't shoplift. Hey, did you see the game on TV Sunday?"

4. Make a joke. "Cheating won't help me understand math. Did you hear the one about (insert funny joke here)?"

5. Keep it simple. "No, thanks. I'm not into that." (Repeat it as much as you need to.)

The Lowdown 77

CLIQUES

"Hey guys, how about giving someone a chance, huh?"

"Trying to break up the cliques would be impossible. It's human nature to group up and that's just what kids do. There's nothing wrong with cliques unless they don't accept others."
—Curtis, 10

"Cliques are lame. All people do is copy each other."
—Andre, 12

Cliques are a part of life. Because there are all kinds of people with different interests, there are many groups—or cliques. Just like Curtis said above, there's nothing *wrong* with cliques themselves. They're just groups of people who like some of the same things. It's when people from cliques tease or act like they're better than others that feelings get hurt.

For example, a group of kids might pick on smaller, taller, shorter, or heavier kids in school, or make fun of people's clothes or hair. When people in cliques see themselves as part of the group and want to fit in, they often feel pressure to copy the behavior of the group—even if it means being mean to others or making them feel left out.

Maybe you sometimes feel that kind of group pressure. You might worry that you'll be left out or teased next if you don't join in. Ask yourself if it's worth it to spend time with a clique that hurts or puts down others. Do you want to have to act in certain ways to be accepted, or just not be yourself? It's a lot more fun to hang out with friends who like the true you.

CHECK THIS OUT

Cliques, Phonies, & Other Baloney by Trevor Romain. Suggestions for dealing with cliques when you're standing on the outside looking in.

78

BULLYING IS NEVER OKAY

> "I was placing my books in my locker when a kid decided I was going to be his punching bag. He slammed me up against the locker and swore at me. A teacher had to step in for my defense."
> —Collin, 13

Bullying is a big problem in many schools. You might know some kids who tease, name call, threaten, or hurt others. Maybe, like Collin, you've had to deal with a bully. Some bullying is public and meant to get attention or laughs from a crowd. It happens out in the open where a lot of people see it. Other times kids bully when no one else is around. They might want to keep it a secret and hold power over another person.

Everyone deserves to be safe, accepted, and respected at school. Bullying is never right and needs to be stopped right away. If you or someone you know is being bullied, talk to an adult right away.

TIPS FOR DEALING WITH BULLIES

1. Don't get physical. More fighting can only make things worse, and you could get hurt.

2. Avoid the person. Try to stay away from situations where you are alone with the bully.

3. Look the person in the eye and say, "Leave me alone" in a confident voice.

4. Stay in groups as much as possible. A lot of the time bullying happens to kids who are alone.

5. Report the bullying. Teachers can help stop bullying. Tell your parents, too.

6. Run if you have to. If you're in a situation where you don't feel safe, get away as fast as possible.

A GUY LIKE YOU

FRANKIE MUNIZ is a hit with teens. His work on TV shows and movies has made his face recognizable all over the world. As Malcolm in the TV show *Malcolm in the Middle*, Frankie plays a genius who's often teased by other kids for being a geek. And in the movie *Agent Cody Banks*, Frankie plays the title role—a teen CIA agent sent to a school to battle bullies on behalf of a classmate. Frankie can relate to some of his roles. He has had his own experience with bullies. Frankie was teased in school for being small—and for being smart. (Like the Malcolm character he plays, Frankie has a very high IQ.) Frankie, though, handled himself well. He says: "I wouldn't let them get to me. I wouldn't retaliate and get mad at them, because I knew that that was what they wanted. I was always getting teased about my height, but hey, I'm short, nothing I can do about it."

GUYS SOUND OFF ON CLIQUES AND BULLYING

SURVEY SAYS...

"Bullying is mean and immature. I think that it happens a lot because kids that don't have friends or get bullied themselves need to feel like they're better than others."
—Jamaal, 12

"Cliques are annoying because all they talk or think about are about themselves. They won't let you join in any games or activities."
—John, 10

"The only problems I have at school are with bullies. But I put out their fire with witty comments."
—Neil, 12

"I really do not like cliques and bullies because they hurt people and make them feel left out. On the other hand, some cliques make a lot of people feel accepted."
—Ricky, 11

"I think that cliques are fine because everyone should have a group of friends to hang out with, but I don't think that bullying is all right."
—Tom, 13

"Bullying should be stopped no matter what it takes."
—Brian, 9

"I usually deal with bullying by walking away. If that doesn't work, I'll just keep saying, 'Leave me alone' until they get bored and stop."
—Chris, 12

"If bullies bother you, tell a teacher. I know that it seems like a lame thing to do, but it is the only way to get him off your back without getting yourself in trouble also."
—Guillermo, 13

"One guy calls me a 'fag' to make me feel bad."
—L.J., 12

GUYS CAN RESOLVE CONFLICTS

"There are lots of arguments about football and other sports we play at school."
—Art, 11

"Sometimes my friends and I play-fight, but it gets out of hand."
—Eric, 13

Conflict is a part of life. You're going to meet people who give you a hard time or don't agree with you. Classmates might insist they're right and you're wrong. Bullies may try to push you around. Problems can come up on the field or court, too. Maybe guys on your team argue about the rules of the game or who should play what position.

It's easy to get upset or angry when you have disagreements. But you can learn to handle tough spots in a smart way. Instead of getting riled up, stay calm and talk with the person (or people) about the conflict. You have a right to give your side of things. Just be sure to listen to theirs, too.

The thing about conflicts is that small ones often become much bigger ones. When people don't stay calm or listen to one another, things can get out of control. If you need to, get the help of an adult at school who can help keep the discussion on track. You'll feel better for dealing with the problem in a mature way.

SPORTSMANSHIP TIPS

1. Treat everyone in the game with respect. Teasing or putting others down is mean, and it can lead to fighting.

2. Play by the rules. Don't cheat or change how the game works part way through.

3. Be a team player. Involve others and share the credit for success. Don't blame a loss on someone who made a mistake.

4. Be a good loser. It's a class act to say, "Congratulations on a great game!" It's not at all classy to insist that the only reason you lost is because the other team cheated.

5. Be a good winner. Resist the urge to brag or gloat. Feel good by being proud of your achievement—not by making others feel bad. Compliment the other team's game.

6. Have fun. Don't forget that it's a game and you're supposed to enjoy yourself.

The Lowdown

ROMANCE

"Girls are usually more mature than guys. Guys always make up stupid jokes and laugh at stuff. Girls all seem too good for that. They seem to grow up faster and grow out of childish stuff."
—Henry, 12

If you're confused about your feelings, talk with an adult you trust.

Changes during puberty can leave you with a lot of mixed-up feelings—including about the opposite sex. Girls are growing into young women before your eyes, and you might start becoming more attracted to them. Maybe girls suddenly seem like great friend material, or people you'd like to know on a more-than-friend basis. If you're like a lot of guys, you might not know where you stand. Maybe you don't know how to act in front of girls or know what to say.

For some guys, girls and romance don't really come into the picture until the higher grades. These guys choose instead to focus on other things, like school and sports. They might think that friendships are great, but that more involved relationships with girls aren't something they're looking for. For other boys, the attraction to girls just isn't there. All of these situations are okay. Adolescence is a time when a lot of guys are still figuring these things out.

OTHER GUYS' THOUGHTS ON GIRLS

"Girls are as fun to hang around with as guys."
—Nate, 11

"People will start dating and doing other things at different ages. I think I'm growing into dating slowly."
—Zach, 12

SURVEY SAYS...

"I think that it is okay to date when you reach a certain age, but not seriously—like fancy dinners or anything. Maybe a movie or something."
—Malcolm, 11

"I don't know how to tell if my girlfriend is cheating on me."
—Pablo, 13

"Dating is nothing. All you have to do is ask someone out and either get accepted or rejected. It's no big deal."
—Leo, 12

"I think dating before seventh grade is stupid. It's cool to hang out with girls as friends, though."
—Tim, 13

"I'd like to know how to keep a conversation going with girls. It seems like I get nervous around them and run out of things to say."
—Tomas, 10

"My girlfriend still thinks we're going out—even though we broke up a long time ago."
—Dave, 11

"I don't know how to talk to girls. I freeze up and don't know what to say."
—Evan, 12

"Girls don't like me."
—Ken, 10

"I like to hang around with girls because some of them are nicer than some boys."
—Rafael, 13

"I have girls who are best friends in my classes. It's great. We talk and that's it."
—Mike, 12

"Sometimes guys feel pressure to act all cool and macho in front of the girls. I think it's dumb."
—Brandon, 11

83 BE A FRIEND FIRST

Like many guys from the survey, I felt awkward around girls during adolescence. I remember when the girls in my class started to wear makeup and perfume. They seemed to be in a different universe than me. They were more mature and confident, and they seemed to know more than I did. To begin a conversation with a girl, I remember having to take a deep breath and get up all of my courage. I was afraid she wouldn't be interested in me.

But in time I grew more comfortable with girls. I realized that in a lot of ways they weren't that different from me. They were going through a lot of changes of their own—like me, they were trying to figure out confusing feelings that come up in adolescence. It turned out that some of my best friends were girls. After I got over my shyness, I realized that we wanted a lot of the same things, including friends we could count on and trust.

If you feel awkward around girls, try just being a friend. Most girls aren't impressed with cheesy jokes or pick-up lines. They'll be happy you're interested in them first as a friend.

No way! That's my favorite movie, too!

CONVERSATION ICE BREAKERS

1. "What's your family like? Do you have brothers or sisters?"

2. "What subjects (or teachers) do you like at school?"

3. "What kind of music (or bands) do you like?"

4. "Do you play sports? Are you in other activities?"

5. "What do you and your friends like to do together?"

6. "What's your favorite movie (TV show)?"

7. "Who's your favorite author?"

8. "What's the coolest place you've ever been?"

9. "What do you like to do outside of school?"

10. "Do you have any pets?"

84

The Lowdown

GOING OUT

As the survey showed, guys have different ideas on going out on dates. Some had already started; others were comfortable waiting for a while. There is no magic age when you're ready—it varies from guy to guy. It may depend a lot on family values and rules, too. Your parents might think it's okay to date now, or maybe they want you to wait. They may say okay to going out in groups to the movies or the mall, but not to spending time alone with a date.

If your parents give the okay to go out, plenty of other questions come up. What will you do? Where will you go? How will you get there? Who pays? You can plan out your date together before the day comes. One impression that a lot of guys get from TV and movies is that they have to be the smooth guy who comes on strong. Fortunately, real life isn't like that and you can cut yourself some slack. You don't have to be Mr.

Cool—just relax and be yourself. That's who your date wants to get to know, after all.

Movies, TV shows, and advertising can also give guys the idea that everyone in the world is having sex. Sometimes the message is that to be a "real man," you have to be sexually active. Maybe you know guys who feel this pressure to brag (or lie) about sex to gain status in the eyes of the group. The truth is that most young people aren't having sex. As you get more dating experience, you and another person *may* want to experiment with kissing and being "physical" in other ways. Remember that all people have their own comfort level and values. Show respect by not pressuring anyone to do something they're not comfortable with. If you're still figuring out what boundaries are right for you, talking things over with an adult you trust can help.

CHECK THIS OUT

The Teenage Guy's Survival Guide by Jeremy Daldry. Info on girls, growing up, and getting along during adolescence. Lots of answers to questions guys have on relationships.

BE YOURSELF

When I was young, I loved books. I liked to play ball with the other kids sometimes, but I also spent a lot of time reading alone. I sometimes felt different from many of the kids on my block—they'd play together all day long. I worried that there was something wrong with me. But I later realized that I was just being myself. It was okay if I spent a lot of time in the new worlds that books opened up to me. Everyone has a different personality and interests. I just happened to really be into books.

Maybe you're someone who likes to spend a lot of time hanging out with large groups—no crowd is too big. Or maybe you're more quiet or shy and prefer spending a lot of time on your own, kind of like I did. You might want to date now. Then again, maybe you'd rather wait until you're older. You might be into music, or snowboarding, or computers, or a collection, or just about anything. The important thing to remember is that as long as you're doing what feels right, you're fine. Surviving the social scene—whether it's friendships, dating, or just choosing how you spend your time—is figuring out what works best for you and going with it. Be comfortable with who you are.

Take Action!

What does it mean for you to "be yourself"? Make a list of things that you think are important. What thoughts, ideas, and actions define you?

FUTURE

 **IT'S YOUR LIFE**

Imagine your life as a movie. You're the main character or hero and family members, friends, and other people you know make up the supporting cast. The storyline includes all of your experiences up until now. There are things you've accomplished, decisions you've made, kind things you've done, and problems you've solved. Some of the things you've done are pretty impressive—other things you'd like to change.

The movie reaches the present and you start thinking about how you want the plot to unfold. Where do you want to go? What kind of hero do you want to become? Imagine the next scenes— your life. You can probably see yourself accomplishing new things—graduating from school, going to college or a tech school, working. Use your imagination to really think about who you want to be and what you'd like to do with your life. Once you've seen the future—what you want—come back to the present. What can you do right now to get to the future you see for yourself?

A GUY LIKE YOU

Come October and the Major League Baseball playoffs, ask New York Yankees fans who they want up to bat and many will say **DEREK JETER**. The Yankees shortstop is known for clutch hits in tight situations—not to mention spectacular plays in the field at key moments.

Derek's success in the major leagues has come after a lot of hard work and concentration on a single goal. While still in Little League, Derek had his eyes set on being the starting Yankees shortstop. He told his dad then that he wanted to play the position for the team, and supported New York throughout middle school by wearing jackets and jerseys. In his eighth grade yearbook, he predicted that in ten years he would be playing for the Yankees. His prediction came true! It's no wonder that today Derek is highly respected by fans and players for his focus and work ethic. They're qualities Derek has used to his advantage from a young age.

Take Action!

Most people don't grow up to be sport stars. But the same determination and hard work you might use to reach the top of your game can be valuable toward reaching other life achievements. Think about where you want to go. What vision do you have for your future? If you like, write in your notebook about what you might like to do and the kind of person you'd like to be.

SOME GUYS' HOPES FOR THE FUTURE

87

"My dad is a scientist and I want to be one, too. It seems like fun work."
—Vince, 12

"I'm not sure what I want to be, but I do want to help in the community. Maybe like a nurse, firefighter, or policeman."
—Bruce, 13

SURVEY SAYS...

"I'd like to be a writer and actor. Plus I want to do cartoon voiceovers. It's cool work."
—Alvin, 10

"I want to be a guy who has a well-paying, steady job and who doesn't sweat the small stuff. I also want to be someone who takes the time to do stuff other than work."
—Boris, 11

"I want to grow up to play football. I want to be one of those people who everyone respects—even players from the other teams."
—Billy, 12

"I'd like to be a comic artist. People have told me that my stuff is good and that if I work hard enough I could be famous."
—Sonny, 11

"I want to be a famous singer with lots of real friends."
—Darren, 13

"I want to be two things as an adult—a painter and a professional violinist."
—Malachi, 12

"I'd like to be a businessman. Life on Wall Street seems exciting."
—Joshua, 11

"I want to be a doctor who helps people get better."
—Chandler, 13

"I want to be a famous soccer player like Ronaldo. But not with his hair!"
—Malik, 13

"I'd like to be a hard worker who likes the job he's doing."
—Rory, 12

"I like computers and want to be a software engineer."
—Tyler, 11

"BMX riding is my favorite thing. I'd like to do it as a professional."
—Dillon, 9

"My grandpa was a lawyer and I want to do that."
—Derek, 10

ASSEMBLY

What about that assembly today, huh?

I don't get it, Tyler.

Why are we supposed to be thinking about careers already? We're only 13!

I know. Seems like there's lots of time to figure things out. But it did get me thinking...

About what?

I've been thinking about being a doctor.

It seems like cool work.

Yeah? I've been thinking about architecture. I love building things. But not only that, I like to draw them out and design them. Architecture's tough though – it takes a lot of school.

Same with being a doctor. That's why I kind of liked the assembly. It helps to think ahead – about classes you might need now to be successful later on.

It makes me think about school differently, too...

Did you hear that stuff about mentors?

Yeah – I never thought about getting one, but now I think it sounds cool.

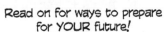

Hey, Jake, you know what? All this heavy thinking is making me hungry.

I'm with you dude. Let's grab some lunch.

Read on for ways to prepare for YOUR future!

99

88 SET GOALS

Some guys have a clear vision for what they want to do when they get older. Others are still figuring it out. Maybe you're more concerned about making the debate or swim team than about what job you'll have as an adult. That's okay. No matter what your interests or wishes for the future, there are things you can do now to get to where you want to go.

One practical way to go about it is by setting goals. Goals are things you want and are willing to work for. There are short-term and long-term goals. Short-term goals can be accomplished pretty quickly. You might have a goal of working out for half an hour today, or finishing your math homework in study hall so that you can hang out with friends tonight.

To accomplish long-term goals, you'll probably have to put in more work over a longer period of time. Long-term goals are those you'd like to achieve in the months and years ahead. Improving your grades, making the varsity tennis squad in high school, and getting into college are all examples of long-term goals.

While you won't be able to accomplish long-term goals overnight, setting up short-term goals that move you toward them is a good way to keep yourself going in the right direction. Not only do you get closer to life plans you have, but you gain confidence. With each new thing you achieve, you can feel good about yourself and better prepared to take on bigger goals.

Think about your long-term goals and make a plan for reaching them. What can you do this week to work toward your goals? This month? This year? Talk with an adult about steps you can take now to help make your life plan a reality.

START SMALL

89

Goals are great for giving you direction and confidence. But some people run into problems when they set goals that are too big or difficult. For example, bringing up a grade in one of your classes can be a really huge challenge. Just saying you want to do it is not going to get you an "A". Instead, you'll need to set up some smaller, short-term goals that can help you develop habits and skills that you'll need to reach your big goal. For example, you could set a goal of getting 100 percent on Friday quizzes, or to improve your class participation. Maybe late (or lost) work is making you lose points. Make it a goal to get organized and plan out your days to get things done on time. Focusing and following through on these short-term goals can help you achieve the larger one of raising your grade. Keep track of your progress on these smaller goals—day by day, week by week—and you might just find yourself having accomplished something very special.

GOAL-SETTING TIPS

1. Make goals reachable. Aiming too high can make it hard to achieve what you want and leave you frustrated.

2. Make goals specific. Instead of "Make more friends," make your goal to join an activity that gives you a chance to meet others.

3. Really believe in your goals. It's hard to work for something you're not sure you want.

4. Have a timeline for accomplishing goals. Specific dates can keep you on track.

5. Keep track of your progress in a notebook. Having goals in writing—and keeping tabs on how you're doing—makes a big difference.

6. Stay positive. Believe you can achieve the goals you've decided on.

7. Tell people about your goals. They may be able to support you in some way. Plus, talking about goals can be a good first step for making them more real to you.

8. Review your goals regularly. Looking at your goals often can keep you focused on what you want.

9. If you stumble, don't give up. Admit to yourself you got off track, but continue trying to achieve goals you've set.

10. When you reach a goal, celebrate your achievement. Even share your victory with others.

GOALS PUT YOU IN CHARGE

Goals can help you take on challenges that come up. I had a learning difference that made it hard for me to read. I made learning to read better my goal, and set up steps to achieve it. I worked on reading for hours and hours, and set up a time after school that I could work with a teacher. It was difficult and took a lot of work, but setting out to do these things—and following through on them—helped me to become a skilled reader.

After I experienced this success, reading became one of my favorite activities. Not only that, but becoming a better reader gave me a lot of confidence, and I started to do better in all of the subjects at school. I also gained courage to try new activities. For example, I joined the school newspaper, which proved to be great experience for the work I eventually did as an adult.

Goals also helped a lot when there were tough times for me at home—including during my parents' divorce. When I felt bad because there were things I could not control, I'd concentrate instead on goals for my schoolwork, interests, and hobbies—things that I could control. It made me feel good to achieve in these areas. And staying focused on what I *could* change kept me moving forward. Instead of letting other people or tough times control my life, I set goals that helped me create my own future.

When have you used goals to overcome a challenge or take control of your life? Write about these times and keep the paper handy so you can remember the impressive ways you've shaped your own life.

The Lowdown

WHEN YOU DON'T REACH GOALS

91

Goals don't always work out—even when you give reaching them your best shot. Maybe you're looking forward to basketball tryouts in the fall. You played on the team last year, and you've put in a lot of time on the court over the summer—playing pick-up games with friends, shooting baskets until it's too dark to see. The big tryout day comes and you freeze—you can't seem to do anything right. Even worse, the other guys seem to have grown a foot since last year and they're running circles around you. You get cut.

End of the line? Not at all. Sure, you might be disappointed when you make mistakes or fail at something. But there are almost always more chances to succeed. The key is to remember that you have to make those chances happen for you. How? Pick yourself up off the floor and make a new plan for reaching your goal.

"You can do it. No matter what anyone says, you can do it."
—Hakim, 12

"Life can be tough, but never stop trying to do your best."
—Arnold, 11

Brainstorm ideas with your friends or parents for getting to where you want to go. You can still play ball, after all, even if you don't make the cut. Join a team at your community center or organize a group of friends. Maybe you can ask a coach for help, or play on the practice squad so that you can improve for next year's tryouts. It might take persistence and determination, but not taking no for an answer can put you in good position to achieve your goals.

EXPLORE YOUR INTERESTS

"I like animals and want to be a veterinarian."
—John, 13

"I'm good at math and science. I want a job where I can use those subjects."
—Pat, 11

One way to help you create your own future is to pursue your passions. Most guys have hobbies and activities they really care about. It's a great quality of adolescence—your attention span gets longer and you can get totally absorbed into particular interests.

What are the things you really like or are good at? It's often these interests that lead you to the kind of work you'll enjoy as an adult. A guy who loves to draw characters or is always copying illustrations from comic books, for example, might turn out to be a cartoonist or illustrator. Someone who's crazy about playing guitar might decide to become a professional musician. Guys who love reading books may want to become writers. Even

when interests don't turn into career paths, you'll still be spending time in fun ways and developing your skills.

It's great to follow interests you have right now, but don't be afraid to try new things, too. Maybe you're interested in camping, hiking, or other outdoor activities, but don't know much about them yet. You might get started by taking a community education class or joining an organization that offers outdoor opportunities. If you're not sure how to pursue a hobby or interest, talk with a teacher or parent about ways you might get going.

A GUY LIKE YOU

R.L. (BOB) STINE, author of the Goosebumps and Fear Street series, loved telling horror stories when he was young. In his boyhood home near Columbus, Ohio, Bob and his brother often tried to scare each other with gory, spine-tingling stories before falling asleep. One night, while trying to put a spook into his brother, Bob stumbled upon an old typewriter in the attic. He instantly wanted it. At seven years old, Bob began typing up comics and funny magazines. He drew the pictures too, and thrilled his junior high friends with the little books. Having a wild imagination for all things frightening and gruesome, it wasn't long before Bob turned from the funny pages to horror stories. All of those frightening bedtime stories shared with his brother have proven to be good material for Bob's many books.

CHECK THESE OUT

YMCA (www.ymca.net). Offering a variety of programs, the Y is a great place to meet up with other guys, get a workout, or take classes on a variety of topics.

Boy Scouts of America (www.scouting.org). Offers lots of exciting outdoor opportunities including hiking, camping, and service projects.

YOU CAN FIND A MENTOR

A great way to develop your interests is by getting a mentor. A mentor can be anyone who supports you as you work toward your goals or teaches you more about the things you like—in or out of school. Many mentors have experience and know-how in certain subject areas and can help you develop your own skills. If you're into computers, for example, you might talk with an expert at school or in your neighborhood.

Mentors can be helpful in nearly any interest or subject. Want to play in a band? You might talk with a local musician or older kids at school. They'll probably have some good advice for you. Maybe you can even sit in on a practice session or attend a concert. Interested in science? You might talk with a teacher at school or look into summer programs in your area. Depending on how serious you are, you might even email someone at a local college or university who can share his or her expertise. Maybe you can spend a day observing what he or she does.

CHECK THESE OUT

Big Brothers Big Sisters of America (www.bbbsa.org). This organization offers one-on-one mentoring for kids ages 5–18. With programs in over 5,000 communities across the country, it's a good bet there are opportunities near you.

Boys and Girls Clubs of America (www.bgca.org). An organization with programs all over the United States. Check your phone book or the Web site for chances to participate in your area.

MENTOR/National Mentoring Partnership (www.mentoring.org). Visit the Web site of this organization to find a mentor in your community.

A GUY LIKE YOU

DENZEL WASHINGTON is one of the biggest stars in Hollywood. Known for keeping his cool and playing a wide variety of characters, he has wowed audiences in films like *Remember the Titans, Antwone Fisher,* and *Malcom X.* Long before his days of lighting up the big screen, though, Denzel was a normal teenager growing up in Mount Vernon, New York. To stay out of trouble, he spent a lot of his time at the Boys and Girls Club of Mount Vernon.

Denzel enjoyed the programs so much that he has joked that staff often had to kick him out of the building at night. Not only did the organization offer Denzel a safe place to have a good time, but it also allowed him to meet Billy Thomas, the director of the Mount Vernon Boys and Girls Club—someone who would be a mentor and an influence on Denzel throughout his life. Denzel Washington credits Billy Thomas with teaching him to believe in himself and work toward his potential.

94

FIND OUT MORE

With a mentor, one of the best ways to learn is by asking questions. Even people you've known for a long time have a lot of know-how they can pass on to you. And new people you meet might be experts in other areas you want to know more about. When you ask questions you show that you're interested in another person's life and work and that you want to learn. You can discover amazing things you've never thought about before—or learn more about something you've already taken a look into. Just asking others about what they do and how they got to where they are today can give you a lot of great information.

Don't be embarrassed to ask questions—or worry that people will think you're clueless. Questions show your intelligence and curiosity.

QUESTIONS FOR MENTORS

1. What is your profession?

2. What made you choose the work you do?

3. How did you get started?

4. What did you study in school?

5. What do you like about your job? What don't you like?

6. Did you have a mentor?

7. How do you stay at the top of your field?

8. What was the biggest mistake you made? What did you learn from it?

9. What are you proud of?

10. What advice do you have for me?

YOU CAN HELP OTHERS—AND YOURSELF

You don't have to be an adult to be a mentor or help others out. There are many things you can do right now to share your knowledge and make a difference in people's lives. Do you remember a time when a buddy was having trouble with a subject in school and you worked to help him understand it better? It probably felt good to see him get it and know that your own abilities helped him along the way. Or maybe there's a neighbor you regularly help with groceries or other errands. You can see the person appreciates your effort—and you can feel proud that you're able to make a difference.

You have a lot to offer. There are many opportunities for you to use your qualities and skills to make others' lives better. Maybe it's visiting older people at a senior center or helping out at a food shelter. You might get involved in an effort to clean up a local park or join a campaign to persuade a politician to solve a problem in the community. Maybe you can help out younger kids at school or in your community by teaching them new things.

These are all small things you can do to make a big difference—and develop your own skills, too. You'll feel good about yourself, learn how to do new things, and gain confidence that can carry over into all of the other parts of your life.

CHECK THESE OUT

Idealist.org (www.idealist.org). This Web site features information on volunteer opportunities, including those especially for young people. Find info for helping out in food shelters, churches, schools, and other places around your neighborhood.

SERVEnet (www.servenet.org). Information on volunteer programs around the United States. Go online and enter your zip code for opportunities in your area.

> "I admire my parents because they lived through hard times and still have a happy life."
> —Jorgé, 12

GUYS CAN FIND HEROES

I worried a lot as a boy about the tough times my family went through. But I would always feel better when I met or read about a person who managed to build a good, successful life—despite facing tough circumstances. I began a "Heroes" file with the stories I cut out of newspapers or magazines about these people. Even though they faced disabilities, sickness, poverty, or other hard conditions, they somehow found a way to switch on a light in themselves and stay strong. Their stories gave me courage and even power to overcome obstacles in my own life.

Look around for the heroes and role models in your life. Who do you look up to and admire? A teacher dedicated to students' learning? A coach committed to fair play and the excellence of the team? An older student who has helped you out? A parent who works long hours and makes personal sacrifices so that you can have a better life?

Some people think that heroes or role models have to be celebrities or sports stars, but that's not true. Many famous people do make a positive impact upon the community and have some great qualities. But there are also lots of people closer to home living good lives that you can learn from. They're often unsung heroes in the community who help make people's lives better through simple actions. Think about the qualities you admire in these people and follow their lead.

CHECK THIS OUT

My Hero (www.myhero.com). Information on a wide variety of people who have achieved great things and made a difference in the world. Log on to the site to nominate your own hero.

GUYS HAVE ROLE MODELS

"My role model is my Big Brother, Jay. He helps me with all of the things in my life and gives good advice."
—Pat, 10

"My stepdad is kind and caring. He has a college degree and is very successful in his work."
—Jim, 12

"My mother works hard and would do anything for us."
—Denny, 13

SURVEY SAYS...

"My dad's a great man with a greater heart."
—Pascal, 10

"I look up to my neighbor. He's a respected doctor."
—Hugh, 12

"My uncle Greg is funny, nice, cool, creative, and treats others the way he wants to be treated."
—Zach, 11

"My grandpa is very wise. He's a retired fireman, too."
—Wallace, 10

"My aunt Logan has very strong faith and always does what's right."
—Mackenzie, 12

"My sister's boyfriend, Scott, is a cool guy. And he has a good head on his shoulders."
—Demetrius, 9

"My role model is my dad because in my opinion he is the best dad ever."
—Joseph, 12

"My best friend, Tom, is a little older than me, but I think he's the best. He's smart, loyal, and brave. He always does the right thing."
—Larry, 11

"I'm my own role model because I'm teaching myself how to live."
—Stewart, 13

BE YOUR OWN HERO

Watching *Spider-Man* and other action movies can be a rush. There are breathtaking shots of characters jumping or flying between buildings, rushing after villains, and saving others. Real people, of course, can't use webs to race through the air at high speeds. But the courage and bravery of these characters is something you can match. You can become your own hero.

How so? Think of all the problems you've faced and overcome. Your family might have been affected by illness or money problems and maybe you stepped up to take on more responsibility—or even got a job to help out. Maybe you weren't feeling your best but played in an important game because you didn't want to let your team down. Or maybe you did the right thing—like standing up for someone who was being picked on. These things take guts and determination.

In real life, there are no superheroes or mutant villains. But you have the chance to do brave things each day. And when tough times or sticky situations come up, you have the skills and courage to take them on.

Take Action!

Think about an achievement that you're proud of. Have you helped someone out or accomplished a big goal? Write about it in a notebook or journal.

99

CREATE A PLAN FOR YOUR LIFE

What do you want in life? Where would you like to be in one year? Five years? Ten? Thinking about your plans for the future can help you remember what's important to you and stay on track. It can be fun to create a "life plan." Who isn't excited about all of the opportunities that come with getting older? You have some great years coming ahead.

Start by thinking about a year from now. What are some of the things you'd like be doing? Do you want to join the swim team? Another activity? Run for class office? Get a job so you can earn some extra money? Write down your goals (see pages 100–103) for your life plan.

Now, think ahead five years. What are some of the things you want to have accomplished? What kinds of school activities or work experience do you want to have? And ten years out. Would you like to be in college? Working? Where? Doing what?

Creating a plan for your life can give you a vision of the future you want for yourself. Remembering your long-term goals regularly will keep you thinking about the steps you can take now to reach them. You may want to change or update your plan and goals as you go along to reflect new interests or changes in your life. That's okay. Goals give you a framework in which to operate; they don't have to stay the same forever.

Think about your life plan. What would you like to achieve? What kind of person do you want to be? Write down some goals you can set to get there.

ADVICE FOR SUCCESS IN THE FUTURE

SURVEY SAYS...

100

"Have fun in life and don't try to grow up too fast."
—Juanito, 11

"Stay in school so you can get a good job."
—Reese, 13

"Keep your head high and never give up. Be proud of who you are."
—Wally, 13

"Have fun in life."
—Alberto, 13

"Have good friends that are honest and true. They can help along the way."
—Joel, 11

"There is not just one thing necessary for success. It depends on lots of things—like having confidence, making good choices, and having computer skills."
—Rufus, 13

"Like my English teacher told me, you don't have to do everything perfect. Just try your best."
—Lyle, 10

"Not being yourself only wastes time and gets you going in the wrong direction. If you stay true to yourself, though, the sky is the limit."
—Marty, 12

"When doing new things, be brave and have courage."
—Rudy, 12

"Don't put too much pressure on yourself. You're perfect the way you are."
—Raheem, 12

"Follow your heart and don't do drugs. Ever!"
—Jessie, 10

"Believe that you're special and that you matter to the world. Never forget that."
—Harrison, 11

"Find something you love to do and find a way to get paid for it."
—Javon, 11

A FINAL THOUGHT:

I've offered a lot of information in this book that I hope will help you. Guys who took the survey had a lot of advice, too. What kind of advice would you give? What's most important to you? I'd be happy to hear from you. Photocopy and fill out the survey on the next two pages and send it to me. Or write with any questions or thoughts you have on being a guy or getting older.

Good luck to you!

Bill Zimmerman
c/o Free Spirit Publishing
217 Fifth Avenue North, Suite 200
Minneapolis, MN 55401-1299
help4kids@freespirit.com

THE GUY SURVEY

ABOUT YOU

Age: _____ Race or Ethnicity: _____

City and State: _____

1. IT'S IMPORTANT FOR A GUY TO BE:
(Check the five that you feel are most important)

☐ SMART

☐ SINCERE (you are honest and mean what you say)

☐ FUNNY

☐ MACHO (you like to act tough)

☐ PATIENT

☐ LOVING (you show others that you care about them)

☐ HELPFUL

☐ SENSITIVE (you understand how you and others feel)

FRIENDLY

☐ BRAVE

☐ ATTRACTIVE

☐ CREATIVE (you like to find new ways of doing things, or you might write or draw)

COOL

☐ INDEPENDENT (you like to do things on your own)

☐ STRONG

☐ KIND

☐ CONFIDENT (you're sure that you can do something)

☐ FAIR

☐ POLITE

☐ LOYAL (you care about your friends and family and watch out for them)

☐ OTHER: _____

2. DO YOU HAVE PROBLEMS AT SCHOOL? (Circle one)

Yes, all the time   Usually   Not very often   Never

Explain:

3. DO YOU FIT IN WITH OTHER KIDS? CAN YOU BE YOURSELF AROUND OTHERS? (Circle one)

Yes, all the time   Usually   Not very often   Never

Explain:

4. DO YOU FEEL PRESSURE FROM OTHER PEOPLE TO BE "TOUGH" OR TO ACT IN A "MANLY" WAY? (Circle one)

Yes, all the time   Usually   Not very often   Never

Explain:

MORE >

5. DO YOU GET ENCOURAGEMENT AND ADVICE FROM YOUR FAMILY AND THE OTHER PEOPLE WHO ARE IMPORTANT TO YOU? (Circle one)

Yes, all the time   Usually   Not very often   Never

Explain:

6. LIST UP TO THREE THINGS THAT YOU WORRY ABOUT A LOT AND COULD USE SOME ADVICE ON.

1)

2)

3)

7. DO YOU FEEL OKAY DISCUSSING PROBLEMS WITH OTHER PEOPLE, OR DO YOU FEEL LIKE YOU HAVE TO "KEEP IT ALL IN"?

IF YOU CAN TALK TO SOMEONE, WHO IS IT?

8. WHAT IS THE MOST IMPORTANT THING THAT ANYONE HAS EVER SAID TO YOU?

WHO SAID IT?

9. WHO DO YOU HOLD UP AS A ROLE MODEL THAT YOU WANT TO BE LIKE?

WHY?

10. WHAT KIND OF PERSON DO YOU WANT TO GROW UP TO BE?

11. WHICH IMPORTANT WORDS WOULD YOU LIKE TO HEAR FROM YOUR FAMILY BUT SO FAR HAVEN'T?

WHO WOULD YOU LIKE TO HEAR THEM FROM?

12. IMAGINE FOR A MOMENT YOU HAVE A SON OF YOUR OWN. WRITE DOWN SOME ADVICE THAT YOU THINK WOULD HELP HIM IN LIFE. THIS MIGHT BE SOMETHING THAT YOU WISH YOU HAD KNOWN GROWING UP.

SOURCES FOR FACTS & INFO

YOU

#3. The "A Guy Like You" sidebar on Spider-Man is based on information in *Comic Book Nation* by Bradford W. Wright (The Johns Hopkins University Press, 2001).

#6. The "Fact" box cites information from "Boys to Men," a study published by Children NOW on September 29, 1999.

#7. "The Boy Code" sidebar is based on information in *Real Boys* by William Pollack (Random House, 1998).

#9. The "A Guy Like You" sidebar on Tony Hawk is based on information in *Hawk: Occupation: Skateboarder* by Tony Hawk with Sean Mortimer (Regan Books, 2000) and a July 1999 ESPN.com article by Ron Buck.

#11. The "Fact" box cites information from the American Academy of Family Physicians (familydoctor.org).

#15. The "A Guy Like You" sidebar on Nelson Mandela is based on information in *Modern African Political Leaders* by R. Kent Rasmussen (Facts on File, 1998) and a July 19, 2003, Associated Press article by Ravi Nessman.

BODY AND MIND

#19. The "A Guy Like You" sidebar on Andy Roddick is based on information on his Web site (www.andyroddick.com) and his profile at Jock-Bio.com (www.jockbio.com). The "Fact" box references information from *My Body, My Self for Boys* by Lynda and Area Madaras (Newmarket Press, 2000).

#20 and #22. The material on puberty is based on information from several resources including *My Body, My Self for Boys* by Lynda and Area Madaras, *From Boys to Men* by Michael Gurian (Price Stern Sloan, 1999), *The Guy Book* by Mavis Jukes (Crown, 2002), and the KidsHealth Web site (www.kidshealth.org), operated by the Nemours Foundation.

#23. The "Fact" box is based on information from several resources including *Why Do They Act That Way?* by David Walsh (Free Press, 2004), *My Body, My Self for Boys* by Lynda and Area Madaras, *From Boys to Men* by Michael Gurian, *The Guy Book* by Mavis Jukes, and the KidsHealth Web site (www.kidshealth.org), operated by the Nemours Foundation.

#28. The dietary information is from several resources including the University of Nebraska Nutrition Education Program (nep.unl. edu), the Media Awareness Network (www. media-awarenss.ca), the U.S. Department of Health and Human Services (www.hhs.gov), the National Hot Dog and Sausage Council (www.hot-dog.org), *Time for Kids* (www.time-forkids.com), and the National Center for Health Education (www.nche.org).

#29. The "A Guy Like You" sidebar on Lance Armstrong is based on information in *It's Not About the Bike* by Lance Armstrong with Sally Jenkins (G.P. Putnam's Sons, 2000).

#30. The dietary and fitness information is from several sources including the National Center for Health Statistics (www.cdc.gov/nchs), the President's Council on Physical Fitness and Sports (www.fitness.gov), and the Nemours Foundation (www.kidshealth.org).

#31. The material on sleep and puberty is based on information from several resources including *My Body, My Self for Boys* by Lynda and Area Madaras, *From Boys to Men* by Michael Gurian, *The Guy Book* by Mavis Jukes, and the KidsHealth Web site (www.kidshealth.org), operated by the Nemours Foundation.

#33. The "Fact" box cites information from the National Institute on Drug Abuse (www.nida.nih.gov).

FAMILY

#40. The "A Guy Like You" sidebar on Daunte Culpepper is based on information in *Daunte Culpepper* by Mark Stewart (Millbrook Press, 2002) and an October 27, 2004, article in *USA Today* by Larry Wiesman.

#43. The "Fact" box cites information from the "Ninth Annual MediaWise Video Game Report Card," published by the National Institute on Media and the Family (www.mediafamily.org) on November 13, 2004.

#47. The "A Guy Like You" sidebar on Albert Pujols is based on information in *Albert the Great* by Bob Rains (Sports Publishing, 2005) and his profile at JockBio.com (www.jockbio.com).

#49. The "A Guy Like You" sidebar on Barack Obama is based on information in *Dreams of My Father*, Obama's memoir (Three Rivers Press, 2004).

SCHOOL

#55. The "A Guy Like You" sidebar on Michael Crichton is based on information found at his Web site (www.crichton-official.com).

#58. The "A Guy Like You" sidebar on Colin Powell is based on information from *My American Journey,* Powell's memoir with Joseph Persico (Random House, 1995), and an online March 2000 Scholastic (scholastic.com) interview.

#62. The "A Guy Like You" sidebar on Dav Pilkey is based on information found at his Web site (pilkey.com). The material on puberty is based on information from several resources including *My Body, My Self* for Boys by Lynda and Area Madaras, *From Boys to Men* by Michael Gurian, *The Guy Book* by Mavis Jukes, and the Kidshealth Web site (www.kidshealth.org), operated by the Nemours Foundation. The "Fact" box cites information from a May 2002 report by the Centers for Disease Control and Prevention (www.cdc.gov).

#65. The information on multiple intelligences is based on theory developed by Howard Gardner in *Frames of Mind* (Basic Books, 2004).

#67. The "A Guy Like You" sidebar on Tiger Woods is based on information in *Tiger Woods* by William C. Durbin (Chelsea House Publishers, 1998); a March 6, 2005, *USA Today* article by Ann Oldenburg; and an August 30, 2004, Associated Press article.

RELATIONSHIPS

#73. The "A Guy Like You" sidebar on Jim Carrey is based on material in *Jim Carrey* by Mary Hughes (Chelsea House Publishers, 1999) and a June 1993 interview in *Saturday Night* magazine.

#78. The "A Guy Like You" sidebar on Frankie Muniz is based on material from *Frankie Muniz* by Mark Beyer (Children's Press, 2002) and a June 10, 2002, BBC interview by Sian Kirwan.

FUTURE

#86. The "A Guy Like You" sidebar on Derek Jeter is based on material in *The Life You Imagine,* a book by Derek Jeter with Jack Curry (Crown, 2000).

#92. The "A Guy Like You" sidebar on R.L. Stine is based on information in *It Came from Ohio!,* Stine's autobiography with Joe Arthur (Scholastic, 1997).

#93. The "A Guy Like You" sidebar on Denzel Washington is based on information in *Denzel Washington* by Anne E. Hill (Chelsea House Publishers, 1999) and a series of public service announcements Washington did for the Boys and Girls Clubs of America.

INDEX

ABOUT THE AUTHOR

Bill Zimmerman has been a journalist and prize-winning newspaper editor for more than 40 years. Much of his work has been directed toward empowering young people and helping families draw closer together. As a senior editor for *Newsday*, one of the largest daily newspapers, he created a regular interactive feature to teach young people about current events that was twice nominated for a Pulitzer Prize. His newspaper work and his books encourage young people to express their thoughts and feelings through writing and to take action in their lives to make the world better. He believes that every small step counts. A father and husband, Bill has mentored and tutored many young people over the years.

Bill's other books include *How to Become an Escape Artist, My Paper Memory Quilt, Lunch Box Letters, How to Tape Instant Oral Biographies, A Book of Questions, Make Beliefs, Make Beliefs for Kids of All Ages, Lifelines, The Little Book of Joy, Dogmas, Cat-e-Chisms, A Book of Sunshine, My Life: An Open Book, Idea Catchers for Kids,* and *Butterfly Wishes.*

His work also has been featured on the *Today Show*, on the acclaimed PBS Ancestors Series, and in the *New York Times*, the *Washington Post*, the *Wall Street Journal, USA Today, Family Circle, Parents, Esquire, Business Week, Essence*, and many other publications.

Bill is available for speaking engagements addressing positive youth development. Visit his Web sites at www.billztreasurechest.com and www.makebeliefscomix.com.

Other Great Books from Free Spirit

Boy v. Girl?
How Gender Shapes Who We Are, What We Want, and How We Get Along
by George Abrahams, Ph.D., and Sheila Ahlbrand

What does it really mean to be a boy or a girl? This book invites young readers to examine gender roles and stereotypes, overcome gender barriers, and be themselves. Written for both boys and girls, *Boy v. Girl?* explores the issues and examines the facts—about hormones, history, laws, and more. It encourages readers to learn who they are, imagine what they can be—and get past those things that get in the way. It helps them make the most of friendships, school, extracurricular activities, and the future, regardless of what sex they are.
For ages 10–15. $14.95; 208 pp.; softcover; illust.; 7" x 9"

Too Old for This, Too Young for That!
Your Survival Guide for the Middle-School Years
by Harriet S. Mosatche, Ph.D., and Karen Unger, M.A.

Finally there's a survival guide for the "tweens." Comprehensive, interactive, friendly, and fun, meticulously researched and developmentally appropriate, this book addresses issues that matter to young people this age. Packed with quizzes, anecdotes, stories, surveys, and more, this is just what boys and girls need to make the most of middle school—and beyond.
For ages 10–14. $14.95; 200 pp.; softcover; illust.; 7" x 9"

No B.O.!
The Head-to-Toe Book of Hygiene for Preteens
by Marguerite Crump, M.A., M.Ed.

Good hygiene can make a big difference in how kids feel about themselves. This frank, humorous book covers the physical changes of puberty and gives tips on caring for oneself. From breakouts to bad breath, body odor to the parts "down there," and, finally, smelly feet, it helps kids know what to do and why. Fascinating facts, friendly suggestions, and funny illustrations combine in a lighthearted approach.
For ages 9–13. $12.95; 128 pp.; softcover; 2-color; illust.; 7" x 9"

To place an order or to request a free catalog of SELF-HELP FOR KIDS® and SELF-HELP FOR TEENS® materials, please write, call, email, or visit our Web site:

Free Spirit Publishing Inc.
217 Fifth Avenue North • Suite 200
Minneapolis, MN 55401-1299
toll-free 800.735.7323
local 612.338.2068
fax 612.337.5050
help4kids@freespirit.com
www.freespirit.com

Parents, caregivers, and youth workers! Visit www.freespirit.com to download a list of questions and prompts you can use with boys reading *100 Things Guys Need to Know*.